A Walk with God

To: Liz
With much love!

Bob Otto

Dr. Robert W. Otto

B&H Bennett & Hastings Publishing

Contents

ACKNOWLEDGEMENTS

This book would not exist unless I had gone to Austria in October 2008. It was there—with my friends Josef and Janice Schutzenhofer—that I began thinking about writing a memoir recounting my life's journey, including my days as a prisoner of war.

Josef was the inspired one. He wanted to create a painting that would thank the American airmen who helped deliver Austria from the Nazis, and he wanted to place that painting where it would be seen by many of the Austrian people. His purpose was to bring harmony, peace and reconciliation to those people who hated the bombing of their country during World War II. Josef painted the portrait of an American airman seen on the back of this book, and arranged for its installation in the headquarters of the Christian Democratic Party in the city of Graz.

I was invited to represent the American airmen on the day the painting was installed. On that day in Austria, I accepted the gifts of honor and respect for these brave men. It was indeed a life changing event for me, as I relived some of those horrible events of the past and my heart felt the pain and agony of those days fade away.

For all of this I owe a great big thank you to Josef, whom I met through the internet when he was researching the airmen, and whose diligence and talent made the entire affair a great success.

Josef also painted the picture on the front cover of this book. He is a renowned artist and one of the most respected in all of Austria. He came to the United States to study art and received his graduate degree from The Maryland Institute College of Arts, before returning to his homeland of Austria.

I am honored to call Josef and his wife, Janice, my friends.

I also want to acknowledge all of my new Austrian friends who blessed me and my children with their friendship and their wonderful hospitality.

These folks are all listed within the pages of this book and I would like to visit with them again one day.

THANKS

I wish to give thanks to my children, Randy Otto, Regina Cox and Robyn Nordsven, for taking the time to go to Austria with me. It would not have been near as nice if I had gone alone.

I want to thank my wife, Mary Ann, for allowing me to travel and leave her home. Her health would not allow her to make the strenuous trip.

And a great big thank you to Ruthie Hopkinson for coming from Connecticut to Washington State to keep Mary Ann company.

Above all, I want to thank Celeste Bennett of Bennett & Hastings Publishing for all of the work she has done to bring this book to reality. Without her it might have ended up in the wastebasket.

THE EARLY YEARS

"Hear, my son, your father's instructions
and do not forsake your mother's teaching"
(Proverbs 1:8)

October can be a cold and miserable month in southern Idaho. And so it was back in 1922, the year I was born. It would be poetic to say I arrived feet first, but I'm not sure that I did. Nevertheless, labor is rarely a walk in the park for mother or child, and this was no exception.

Most women gave birth at home in those days, with neither a midwife nor a doctor to assist. Our small town had no hospital and only one doctor, and reaching him could be problematic: there were no telephones in the countryside, so contacting the doctor meant driving into town, hoping the doctor was not out on a house call.

My birth would be my mother's third, and my parents knew how difficult childbirth was for her. When Mother felt the birth pangs heralding my arrival, Dad hurried to town to fetch the doctor. Fortunately, the doctor was in. He hurriedly put on his heavy coat, grabbed his medical bag and jumped in his old car to follow my Dad home. They arrived in time.

I don't recall much about being born, but I do remember one of my uncles telling me later that I was a worrisome infant. He told me that I would periodically stop breathing, or as he put it "hold my breath until I turned blue." Someone would then grab me and run outside, where I would take a deep breath as the cold air hit my little body. My blue period lasted only a short while. My mother breast fed me, and I grew rapidly into a tiger of a kid; very active.

The 1920s and '30s were very difficult years for America. Southern states were devastated by dust storms and the crop losses. Most people were out of work. Our family lived on a farm, where life was—to say the least—a struggle. Food was always on the table though, because we raised crops and livestock, and wild pheasants were plentiful in the fields. No one starved, but our survival required diligence.

Farmers did not check in with a time clock: the days began early and didn't end 'til after sundown. The work was demanding, and many a farmer's life ended early due to a heart attack. Our farming implements were pulled by horses when I was a boy, and early in life I learned how to care for our horses and milk our cows. Not many kids have that opportunity anymore. I loved living on the farm. It required hard work, but I thought it well worth our effort—even before we ever had a tractor.

In those years, electricity wasn't available in the countryside. People used kerosene lamps and candles for lighting. Plumbed bathrooms were rare: we had an outhouse, which really was out back. Our house was heated by a woodstove, which my mother also used for cooking. It sounds primitive now, but we had nothing better to compare it to and everyone was in the same situation.

Winters brought plenty of snow, and it was wonderful to come in out of the cold and stand near that old kitchen stove, warming myself and savoring the aroma of fresh bread baking within it. My childhood memories are still pleasantly stirred as I recall coming home from school to find Mother's delicious hot bread, already buttered for me. What a treat!

My early memories of Mother almost always involve seeing her in the kitchen. Two or three times a day she was feeding our family and two or three hired men. When she wasn't cooking she was washing clothes on the old scrub board or ironing with a heavy iron heated on the stove top. But, even with all of the tasks she handled, she always had time for her kids. She was the one we would run to with any little hurt. It was her love and concern that conquered our distress and brought comfort back into the picture. She was a wonderful mother.

Life was not easy and money was not plentiful in those early years, but Mother managed with what we had. In time it took its toll upon her life. One time my dad had to go down to the local jail and bail out one of our hired men who had been tossed in the clink for disturbing the peace as well as another man's face while drunk. It cost fifty dollars to get him out. My mom got very mad at my dad for spending that amount of money when things were so hard. This was the only time I ever saw Mother get really angry. She thought the young man should have stayed in jail for ten days to be taught a lesson. I think the reason my dad got him out of jail was because there was work to do, and he was the son of one of our close neighbors.

In 1926 my dad went into bankruptcy. It was a terrible year, and the crops were not doing very well. He lost the farm. He did not give up, however, and soon he was able to purchase a larger farm close by. It had a big, rock house that had a plumbed, indoor bathroom and a floor furnace fueled by coal. Life began to get easier.

When electricity came to the farm my dad bought mom a real electric washing machine. It was a Maytag, with a ringer on the top to squeeze the water out of all the clothes before they were hung on a line in the sunshine to dry. No more scrub boards! I can't imagine how difficult it must have been to get old dirty, grease stained overalls clean on a scrub board. Not only that, it was hard on the hands and knuckles. My mom never complained.

Electricity also brought a radio to our home along with electric lights. What a change! Reading became a pleasure instead of a struggle, as it had been under the limited lights of the past. Dad even electrified our basement furnace by installing a coal hopper and feeder so we didn't have to go downstairs every now and then to stuff coal into the furnace.

I loved that old, rock house. Recently we returned to the old place: the house is still standing and looking solid as ever. The big barn I recall from my youth has been replaced with a more modern barn and outbuildings. Other than that, it looks about the same, and visiting brought back many good memories.

When I was about eight or nine years old, my dad gave me an old horse. Her name was Topsy. Dad wanted to retire her from hard labor but did not want to sell her, so he gave her to me. She wasn't much; just an old worn out workhorse, slightly sway-back and spavined in all four legs, which means her legs were about to give out. She walked very slowly and sometimes with a limp or two. In spite of all these ailments, she seemed to me like the greatest horse in the world! I took care of her with such loving tenderness that, if my mom hadn't been in charge, I would have slept in her stall.

We didn't have any saddles or fancy bridles at the time, so I would just put on her old work bridle with the blinders on each side, and away we would go. To mount her, I would have to lead her up to the fence or a stump in the yard, or over to the water trough, and then jump on her. She was a very gentle soul and put up with me without getting upset. It was just good to have a horse I could call my own. We got along just marvelously. A boy and his horse.

Topsy was a fairly large horse, without too much finesse or style, and because of her ancient legs she would sometimes stumble and nearly fall down. Her occasional clumsiness, didn't stop this young rider, who was so little his legs barely hung down to the middle of Topsy's rib cage. We had a good time together every day, Topsy and me; a cowboy and his mount. We would trot all around the farm, wherever there was a trail. I knew better than to take her out into the fields and trample down the crops: that would have been the end of my career as a cowboy!

There was only one occasion when I fell off. My next door neighbor, Mitch, and I were riding on Topsy together. Mitch was a few years older than I. We were having a grand time, singing and having fun when something spooked Topsy. We both fell off, with Mitch on top of me. We got up, and my arm was killing me! I was crying up a storm over the pain. What would you expect of a young cowboy? I got home, and as soon as my father saw me, he knew I had a broken arm. He bundled me up with a pillow under my arm and drove me fifteen miles to the nearest hospital.

I remember Dr. Zeller well. He was a tall, thin, hawk-faced man with a slight stoop to his shoulders and a cigar almost always protruding from his mouth. When he didn't have a cigar in his mouth he was usually whistling. He was good, too. In fact, his whistling was one of the things I admired about him. When you stepped into his office and he wasn't busy with a patient you could hear his whistle coming from the inner sanctum. Now, as I look back some seventy years later, there were other qualities about him that went along with the lifestyle of the early 20th century country doctor: he was robust and always willing to make a house call, no matter how far out in the country you lived. Oftentimes he was called out in the middle of the night to care for a sick child or a pregnant lady. Regardless of how blustery the weather or how high the snowdrifts he would bundle up and be on his way.

Dr. Zeller took a look at my arm and loudly announced, "Sure enough, it is broken." We were in the surgery room. Dr. Zeller told my dad to stand behind me, put his arms round my chest and hold on tight. The doctor took hold of my arm from the front side, gave a jerk and said, "There we got it back in place. Now I will put a plaster cast on it." It was a mid-shaft fracture of the humerus. The procedure was very painful for an instant, and then it was all over. I had to wear the cast for six weeks.

During this time I was not allowed to ride Topsy so I just took good care of her with a curry comb every day and good food to eat. She enjoyed every moment of this time. I think she was glad we weren't out trotting around the farm.

One morning I went out to feed and take care of her and there in the middle of the corral lay my beautiful steed, stiff and cold. She was dead. My heart broke as I put my arms around her neck. I poured out my heart and a bucket full of tears. She wasn't much. Just an old worn out workhorse, but to me she was a mighty fine animal. I had chased bad guys and rounded up cattle with her, a four-legged warrior. Now she was gone. Farewell, faithful Topsy.

In the 1930s my dad bought a flock of sheep with one of our neighbors. We built sheep sheds to keep the new mothers and their babies warm as they lambed out in February. A year later, my dad bought out his partner and bought more sheep. For a few years he had 3,000 head of sheep. In the winter, we would lamb them out, and in the early spring they would be driven out to the desert, where spring grass was plentiful and tender. They would slowly work their way through the desert to the mountains, where they would spend the summer. The sheep were kept in two bands of 1,500 each, with a sheepherder to care for each herd. Each sheepherder had a camp wagon, a supply wagon, two workhorses and one saddle horse, plus two or three sheep dogs.

One day, a dog of my own turned up. Rex found us. We woke up, and there he was—asleep on our back porch, a matted bundle of brown and black with a touch of white here and there. He was so skinny his ribs were protruding, and his eyes were sunken into their sockets. He brought to mind a sailor who had been lost at sea for a very long time.

The conversation around the breakfast table that morning went something like this:

"Where do you suppose he came from?"

"I don't have any idea."

"He must have drifted in from some faraway place, from the way he looks."

Mother immediately brought a bottle of milk from the icebox, poured it into a dish, set it on the floor near the dog, then stepped back. The poor dog rushed over and lapped it up as though he hadn't had anything to eat in a very long time. And looking at him, it was obviously true.

Our entire family was immediately attracted to him. Everyone seemed to have a soft spot in his heart for this old stray dog. No one was anxious to get rid of him. It only took a few days for this debilitated animal to respond to milk and table scraps and gain back his strength. We cleaned him up and soon he was following us to the barn each morning as we milked the cows. He didn't mind waiting for someone to squirt warm, fresh milk into his mouth. He soon became the favorite of the whole family.

Once he had gained his weight back and the sheen returned to his hair coat he took on a regal look. That was when we decided to call him Rex. He was a king. All summer long he would follow us to the fields. While we were hoeing beans he would rest quietly at the end of the row. As we would walk back to him he would look up and seem to ask, "What in the world are you guys doing?"

Rex loved to play with kids. He and I became great friends. All day long he would follow me. Many days we would lay down along a ditch bank, look up into the sky and watch the clouds drifting by. I don't know that Rex thought much about the clouds, but he did seem quite content. We would stay there a long time, dreaming dreams. Rex never revealed any of his dreams to me. We would watch airplanes flying by and wonder where they were going, and imagine we were going along with them to some faraway place.

That summer, we had the most fun during haying time. We didn't have a hay bailer then. Rather, all of the hay was raked by hand, into piles that were left to dry. Once that was done, it was time to make haystacks. We would pull a hay sled along the rows, stacking each pile onto the sled then hauling the load to the stacking area. At that point, a derrick pulled the hay off the sled and dumped it on the haystack, where a couple of guys would use rakes to spread it out. That particular summer our hay fields were full of mice, more than usual. They would be hiding under the hay in the fields, and when the hay was picked up the mice would zip around in all directions. Rex would have a picnic! He enjoyed chasing those little creatures and killing, but never eating, them. The cats ate them: they had a field day that summer and grew fat and sassy.

Rex became the protector of our farm. Whenever anyone drove into the driveway he was there to greet them with a ferocious bark. No one could come around without Rex knowing about it and warning the family. At 45 to 50 pounds, he was big enough to back up his bark, although we never saw him bite anyone. People, however, usually stayed in their car until someone came to escort them into the house. When Rex curled his upper lip, bared his teeth and growled it was enough to scare almost anyone.

Rex seemed to have a sixth sense when it came to traveling salesmen. He would be even more persistent in holding them at bay. One old gentleman called on a rather regular basis. We knew him as Grandpa Bridgeman. He sold Raleigh products door-to-door: spices, extracts and other household goodies. Despite Rex, Grandpa Bridgeman never got discouraged, and despite all of the years he stopped by Grandpa Bridgeman never made friends with Rex.

Rex became very useful around the farm. He had a good herding instinct and was helpful in working with the cows and sheep. In the fall of the year when the sheepherders would bring their flocks home for the lambing season, Rex was there to greet them.

I remember two whom we kept in touch with for several years after my dad gave up the sheep business: Daryl Farmer and a man named Sid. These men were both married and their wives went with them in the sheep wagons. Those ladies were brave souls who loved the outdoors! They would park their sheep camps (their living quarters) in the farmyard, bringing their herd dogs with them.

Those dogs soon learned that Rex was in charge of the farm. He didn't take any disrespect. It was his territory. Generally they all got along quite well.

We never knew Rex's age. He came to us when he was full grown, and he was very secretive about his past. After he had been with us for quite some time, he had a severe seizure. He collapsed on his side, chomped his teeth and drooled for a short period of time. Then it was over. He returned to normal, but the seizures returned on occasion. Sometimes he would lose control of his bladder or his bowels. These epileptic type seizures may have been the result of having had distemper at some time. We never knew. We never felt that Rex was dangerous during these periods. He always seemed to be sorry after these episodes.

Rex left our lives just as suddenly as he had entered. One morning there was no Rex around. We called, but he didn't come. One of my brothers found him in our grove of trees. He was dead. You could see where he had thrashed around during the night. The seizures had finally ended his life.

Rex had been a great companion over the years: friend, guard dog and worker around the farm. It was a very sad day for all the family when we found him lifeless. We buried him carefully among the trees and placed a small marker over his grave with his name, "Rex."

Lambing season always brought new life to the farm. Sometimes, in cases when the mother died or didn't have any milk, we would have to bottle feed the lambs. We called them "bum" lambs. It was my job to take care of the little fellows. I would get up early in the mornings, help milk cows and then feed the bum lambs. It was a fun job. At first we had three or four bums, but it grew to be quite a large number. One winter we had eighty-four little lambs needing care. It almost became a full-time job. To cope with the demand, my dad designed a bucket with eight little spigots, a nipple attached to each spigot. Eight lambs suckling at one bucket considerably eased my workload. What fun it was to feed them, watching their little tails switch back and forth as they guzzled the milk! They seemed happy and contented, and they grew rapidly. They became almost pets, and it was hard to part with them as they grew and finally were able to mix with the other sheep.

When spring came, and all the lambs were bigger, it became time to herd them out into the desert. The drive through the desert was over sixty miles and took a couple months. When the weather warmed enough we would hire a sheep shearing crew to come out to the desert. These shearers had all the necessary equipment, including holding pens. There were usually four or five men shearing and two or three men catching sheep and delivering them to the shearer. A good sheep shearer could shave a hundred head a day. It appeared to me to be a backbreaking occupation. The wool would be collected from each sheep, bundled up and tied with string, then put into a huge bag. This bag was suspended from a platform that was about eight feet tall. The platform had four legs, and the top had a hole about two feet in diameter. My job was to tromp the wool down, compacting it as much as possible before it was pitched into the bag. This was sweat-producing work; hard and dirty. When all the sheep were sheared and turned back into the desert, the bags of wool were loaded and taken to a train station for shipment to the woolen mills. There, our sheep's wool would be transformed into woolen blankets, shirts, coats, etc.

It was another twenty to fifty miles to the mountain range where our sheep spent the latter summer months and early fall. All of this land was under the Bureau of Land Management, which granted us permission to take the sheep there and, in the mountains, assigned certain areas to each rancher. I think there was a small charge.

One summer I spent a few weeks in the mountains with Jess, one of the herders. Jess was half Native American Indian, a middle-aged man who had come out from Virginia. That summer was a fun time. There was a bear that was killing our sheep so Jess took some logs and piled them up in the form of a "V." Then he put a dead sheep in the bottom part of the "V," anchored a rifle in the logs and attached a small rope between the trigger of the gun and the carcass of the sheep. That night we heard the gun go off, and the next morning we found the dead bear. That was the last time that summer a bear came around.

Jess was a good cook. He knew how to prepare a whole meal in a Dutch oven, which is a heavy, cast iron pot with a solid lid. He would mix up a whole pot of stew, build a nice fire, put the pot in the middle of it and add more wood on top, then head out to the fields for the day. The fire would burn all day, and the food would be ready by evening. He could bake bread the same way. Bakery sourdough bread cannot compare with bread out of a Dutch oven!

Living in the mountains in a tent was pretty much roughing it. Water was scarce, so we used it sparingly. Fortunately, there were streams, and we used them for drinking water and bathing. Ooooh that water was cold! In those days it wasn't common knowledge that a person might catch a disease by drinking out of mountain streams, and we never did.

I enjoyed my time with Jess, who worked for my dad a number of years. I packed additional self-sufficiency into my survival kit during those days on the mountain with him. Jess was a good man who had very little education. He always told me, "Get an education. You won't get anywhere without a college degree." Quite a few years later I took his advice, and it was good.

I recall a beautiful summer day when the mountains stood guard over the valley, where Dad, Jess and I were going fishing. We were headed to Smiley Creek, which is over Galena Summit, about sixty miles north of Ketchum, Idaho and just before the little town of Stanley. There were still a few patches of snow on the highest elevations, but it was warm down along the streams where the sunshine would pour out upon us.

Our sheep were grazing in a meadow in another valley. We had spent the night in that valley, in a tepee where Jess was camped. My dad and I were taking a few hours off to see if we could catch a salmon before heading home: it would be a great day if we could take a big fish home to my mother!

We gathered our gear at a little store owned and operated by Mr. Bell, an old sourdough whom everyone respected. No one knew his first name: he was always "Mr. Bell." He was a lean, leathery, old man with gray hair, and a crooked pipe perpetually present beneath his bushy, white, mustache.

Mr. Bell spent summers in his own little, log cabin up in the valley. All we had to do was ask, and he would tell us where the salmon were running.

Mr. Bell had been around during the early days of the gold rush, when the valley was overrun with eager miners, anxious for a real strike. At one time the area we were in was well known for gold dredged from its rivers, much as the area around Hailey was known for gold and silver mined from the mountains. The gold dredges were monstrous machines that dug rocks and sand out of the riverbeds, ran them up a belt, sifted the fine sand and gold from the larger rock, deposited the rocks along the river bank, and then moved another few feet to dig some more. Their tailings of rock were an eyesore in pristine countryside and a testimony to the ugly consequences of greed. Since most of the gold is gone and what is left is not worth the effort to retrieve it, the dredges now sit rusting away in peace and quiet among the piles of rock they once dug out of the riverbeds and discarded.

After enjoying some conversation, and a cup or two of java for the adults, we piled into the pickup and drove up Smiley Creek. In those days it was legal to spear fish for salmon. I thought it was an exciting way to catch these big fish. We carried spears with long handles, maybe six to eight feet in length. On the business end of the handle was a sharp metal point with an extension on one side that allowed the spear to go into the fish but prevented the fish from swimming off the end of the spear. The object was to walk along the bank of the creek until you spotted a salmon lolling around in a deep pool or swimming over some shallow rapids, then try to spear him quickly and quietly. It sounds easy, but I learned it took some expertise to be able to hit the target.

Jess, over the years, had, become very adept at this avocation. He made it look easy as he quickly cast his spear into a large salmon. I tried it in a deeper pool down the stream and immediately fell into the water. The icy water was coming straight off a glacier, and I came up gasping for breath. I jumped onto the bank and grabbed the spear for another try.

The time went by rapidly, and before I knew it the day had gone. Jess had to get back to the sheep camp, and we had to head for home. Our catch for the day was three fish, none caught by me. Nevertheless, I was anxious to give it another try one day soon. It had been a wonderful day.

It was always fun when I was out with my dad. He was not only a hard-working farmer/sheepman, he was fun! Being the youngest of his brood, I often got to go with him while my brothers were working on the farm. Those were times of great enjoyment for me.

My father had come to Idaho in the early years of the twentieth century, which were filled with expectations and the possibility of great adventure. Many exciting things were happening in the western part of the United States. The gold rush seemed to be over, but the government was giving land to those who were willing to carve out a homestead from the raw land, whether sagebrush, desert or forest. Opportunity existed for those willing to take a chance, betting their lives and plenty of hard work to build a place of their own.

That was the promise that beckoned when my dad prepared to leave the farm in Wisconsin and take his chances in the west. All he knew was what he had read about it in the papers and tidbits he had heard passed around from the stories told by someone who had been there and returned. But, it didn't make any difference, he was in his early twenties and his mind was made up. Were his mother and dad worried about him going so far from home? Of course they were: how would they know what was happening to him? When would they hear from him?

He knew he couldn't go that far alone, so a friend name Erv Sneeberger decided to go along to explore the possibilities. They both had a few dollars in their pockets and a deep desire to travel and explore the unknown. They climbed aboard a train and headed west.

It was 1909, and the railroad got them all the way to Shoshone, Idaho. Somehow they found their way to Jerome, about fifteen miles away from Shoshone. Jerome had a few wooden buildings along a street that alternated between dust and mud, depending on the season. It wasn't much to look at, but who cared? Beyond the one block main street were a few shanties and tents, the living quarters of a few hardy souls. Beyond that enclave there was nothing but sagebrush as far as the eye could see, though on a clear day they said you could see mountains in the distant north. With the optimism of the pioneer they thought maybe it wasn't all that bad. With a lot of hard work it would be possible to make something out of nothing.

My dad, short on money, went to work for a group of men who were clearing sagebrush. Others set to work building canals, to capture some of the water flowing down the Snake River and establish irrigation for their future farms. All the jobs required plain, hard, manual labor. My father was strong and muscular. In his first job he lead a team of horses to grub away the sagebrush. Next, they gave him a fresno, a large metal scoop with a handle, used to level the land. His job was to fill and then dump it, using the handle to tip it up. It was weary work from daybreak till dark. There wasn't much to do except work. Eventually, they gave him a larger fresno and four horses to pull it.

Although the workdays must have seemed endless, it wasn't long before my father had accumulated enough money to buy his own team of horses and prepare his own land. Once that was done and the canals completed, it was a matter of waiting for the water to start flowing. Then the prepared land could be irrigated. This was rich soil with one drawback: there were lots of rocks. That whole area of Idaho was built upon a giant lava flow that had solidified. In some areas, for miles there was nothing but massive, rocky areas. Most of this land was north of Jerome.

The land my dad was given to farm was quite productive. The first thing he did was to build a small home. About this time, Erv Sneeberger decided he had experienced enough hard work and blazing sun, so he headed back to Wisconsin. As time went by others came from all areas of the eastern and midwest part of the country. Soon a farming community was established. A few years later my dad bought some more land and built a two story house that was quite nice.

A family from Oklahoma homesteaded some land a few miles away. They had traveled from Oklahoma to Oregon in the early 1900s and later decided to come to Idaho by wagon train. This family had seven kids, three boys and four girls. One of them became my mother. Yes, my mom was a pioneer woman who had ventured into the unknown with her family, a young teenager when they arrived in Oregon. They came part of the way on the Old Oregon Trail. I have visited the place where they settled in Oregon, and it looked pretty nice to me. I don't know why they came back to Idaho—as they passed that way before and knew it was nothing but sagebrush—but I am glad they did, as that is where she met my dad. She was in her late teens as they moved to Idaho.

Maybe it was love at first sight. We were never told, but it wasn't too long until he was asking my grandpa if he could marry his daughter. Permission was granted, and in 1912 they were married. He was twenty-six and she was nineteen. In 1913 their first son was born. The next one came along in 1916, and then I was born in 1922. In 1933 my mother had twin baby boys. They were named Richard and Russell. They only lived a day or so. I remember it well. It took Mother quite awhile to recover from the loss of her two little babies.

Sometimes my mom would come along when my dad and I went out on an adventure. She loved the outdoors and didn't mind sleeping on the ground in a tepee, washing in a cold creek and cooking meals over an open fire.

One weekend Dad, Mom and I went out to one of the sheep camps to deliver food for the herder and hay and oats for the horses. It was a warm, clear day and Mom was doing some cooking in the camp wagon. She was bending over the stove, looking into the oven, with her backside out the door of the camp wagon. Out of the blue we heard a shotgun fire, and my mom jumped like she had been shot. Sure enough, that is exactly what had happened! A guy was hunting birds, and they had flown in our direction. We rushed Mom to a doctor's office where he checked her over and picked out a number of buckshot from her bottom. We drove her home, as she sat gently perched in our old pickup truck.

My dad was a very hard worker all the days of his life. His accomplishments were quite remarkable, as he had only an eighth grade education. Our large, old farm was quite productive. We raised 100 acres of alfalfa, many acres of potatoes and sugar beets, beans and grain.

When the lambs grew big enough it became time to separate them from their mothers and ship them off to market. This meant driving them down to the rail head, where the train would stop. There, they were herded into pens, then separated from the band and loaded into boxcars headed for Chicago or some other city. The market for lamb was very good in those days. Over time, it became less lucrative, and when the Union Pacific built Sun Valley, my dad's permit to run sheep on that mountain was canceled. That helped get him out of the sheep business: no range to herd them on during the summertime.

We were the last of a great breed of pioneers who enjoyed some of the more primitive types of outdoor activities. Some of this blood flows slowly in my veins. Dad and I would, from time to time, go fishing for trout in the rivers where some areas allowed only fly fishing. The Big Wood River, which flows down from Galena Summit through Ketchum, Hailey and Bellevue, was once filled with fish. In the days of my youth we would often see a bear along the streams doing his own fishing. Elk and deer would be munching grass in the meadows and beavers were forever building their dams in the creeks. Eagles were plentiful, as they plied the airways searching for their own meals of fish or little varmints. In the past few years fishing in Idaho has become a sport of the past. Many streams are closed to fishing because of the influx of so many people. Those were great days that are gone forever in the valleys and mountains of Idaho.

· 2 ·

THE BETWEEN YEARS

"Trust in the Lord with all of your heart,
and do not lean on your own understanding"
(Proverbs 2:5-6)

Life was pretty good when I was a small kid, and it wasn't always work. We had neighbors with kids about my age, so we would get together and go swimming in the canals. We called it "skinny dipping." There were neighbor girls who liked to swim in the canals too, always alone, with no boys allowed. They were skinny dipping too, and as often as possible we boys tried to spy on them. Pretty exciting stuff for our age. One night my older brother and I, along with a couple of other fellows and a few girls, went skinny dipping together. My brother always denied this sort of thing ever happened. But, it was the truth. Our mother never found out about that excursion. Nor, later, did my wife. Secrets sometimes avoid disaster.

In the winter there was never any lack of snow: we could ice skate on the canals and ski behind cars as they buzzed down the road. With the snow came wind, which would create great snowdrifts. Sometimes the roads would be so blocked by snow that cars could not get through. Many winters school had to be postponed due to the snow, but one year we got lucky. That year, the snow made the roads impassable for cars, but our neighbor brought his horse-drawn sleigh around for all the kids. We'd cover up with a nice, heavy blanket and enjoy every minute of the four-mile ride to school.

I still remember some of my grade school teachers. Miss Graves, my first grade teacher, would not stand for any foolishness. If you acted up, she would come by your desk and give you a crack on the knuckles with a ruler. I had my share of whacks. Miss Dunagan taught my second grade year. She was an easygoing lady who seemed to love all the kids, and every kid felt the same about her. Miss Brown taught our third grade class. She had a happy spirit that reached out to every little kid in the class. My fifth grade teacher was quite young and pretty, and she was an excellent teacher. Everyone, at least all of the boys, had a crush on the aptly named Miss Love.

I remember our grade school principal but not his name. He was a strict disciplinarian. If we caused trouble in class, it was off to the Principals' Office! If there were two of us (boys of course) he would listen to what we were up to and then deal out the punishment. If we had been doing something serious he would give each one of us a paddle and then say, "I want you to give each other a couple of whacks on the bottom. Bend over." That usually settled the problem. It was quite an effective method for keeping us young boys out of trouble. The girls didn't seem to have this type of problem.

My grade school clothes often had patches on them, and my socks were darned whenever a hole appeared. That was acceptable, as every other boy in school wore patched pants and shoes with holes in the sole. In those early years we were poor, but we didn't know we were poor.

I had my share of scraps in school and on the playground. Maybe I thought I was bigger than the other kid, or maybe just tougher. At any rate, every once in a while I was in a schoolyard tussle. Sometimes there were bloody noses, but mostly it was a lot of bluff, settled when the playground monitor came around and made us shake hands and forgive one another.

My two brothers seemed to get through their young years and the teens without too much trauma to their bodies. Not me. It seemed as though there was always something coming along to get me. If it wasn't broken arms then it was measles, chickenpox, shingles and a few other maladies. When I had the shingles the doctor said to keep me in bed and put a hot mustard plaster on my back. I don't know which hurt more, the shingles or the treatment. A sadist must have figured out that treatment! Thank goodness they don't use mustard plasters anymore.

Grade school went from first to eighth grade and then we were ready for high school. About this time my mother and I both came down with tonsillitis. We rushed in to see our old friend, Dr. Zeller. He looked at our throats and said, "Those tonsils have to come out." He took my mom in first and then it was my turn. Into the surgery I went. They placed the ether mask over my face, and I soon dozed off. When I awoke, my tonsils were gone and we were ready to go home. I had a terribly sore throat, and I think my Mom did too, but she didn't have time to worry about such things. She had dinner to prepare for our family and a couple of hired hands.

My mom saw me through all of these calamities with tender loving care. I stand amazed at her strength and her determination to not let anything get her down. In the 1930s my mom developed a goiter. She had a large swelling in her neck that required surgical intervention. We were very worried about her, as there weren't many surgeons in our area. Old Doc Dill from Shoshone was one that my dad thought capable of performing the surgery. He did, and it was a success. Mom was out of action for a while, but she bounced back quickly. Mom had that bounce back ability. Perhaps some of it came out of necessity, but I really believe the Lord made her that way so she could pass on some of those qualities to her offspring.

Although I could not see where the path was leading, entering high school was a significant step forward in my progress towards an active spiritual life, and it was a lot of fun.

I really enjoyed high school. The subjects that I enjoyed most were history, biology and Spanish. I never learned how to speak Spanish, which was not the fault of our teacher, Miss Wilson. Mathematics was not on my A-list for anything: it was always a tough subject for me. On the other hand, I liked chemistry.

With some grade school band experience I stepped into the high school band as a trumpet player. That didn't go so well, so I switched to the clarinet and then the saxophone. This was a keeper! For four years I played the baritone sax. We had a great time, especially when we were involved in marching contests with schools from neighboring towns. Every school had handsome uniforms and every school was proud of theirs.

Besides being in the band, I was on the committee that produced our yearbook. I tried out for all of the sports offered … and usually failed. I was not big enough for football, or basketball, or track; all the sports there were at our school. From there on in I had to transfer my potential to girls. That was easy: I liked girls! I thought they must have been put on this earth just so boys could fall for them. I, on the other hand, may not have been in the same category for girls. Fortunately, I never had any problem finding dates for the dances, which were always fun for everyone.

School dances were usually held on the basketball court, carefully supervised by a host of teachers and oftentimes chaperoned by parents. In addition, most of my friends were members of the Mormon Church, and they held weekly dances, where they welcomed me. Then I fell in love, or so I thought, with a girl in a class a couple of years behind ours: I was a senior and she was a sophomore.

She was the pianist at our local Baptist Church. I had never been much of a churchgoer until we met. From that time on I was in church every Sunday morning and Wednesday evening. I'm not saying our Heavenly Father lured me into that church, but if libido were bread crumbs I was a bird who followed Hansel and Gretl's path into the woods. Fortunately for me, it was a heavenly mansion that I discovered at the end of that trail.

It was a small church with an exceptionally friendly congregation. One week, an evangelist visited. His name was Reverend J.B. Long, and one night, near the end of Reverend Long's time with us, I was touched mightily by the Lord. He got me right up out of my seat and marched me to the front of the church, where I knelt and gave my life to Jesus. From that day on, I have never been the same. God has directed and protected me all of these years.

I am forever grateful to that little church, a powerful evangelist who was instrumental in my conversion, and the Lord who empowered him. That date was December 3, 1939. I was seventeen years old. I still have my Bible, with this information written in it.

When I graduated it was off to college for me, but I looked forward to the times when I could come home for a visit. One summer my girlfriend entered the Miss Jerome contest and won. She was then eligible for the Miss Idaho contest to be held at Sun Valley later in the summer. When the time came I drove her and her mother to the contest in Sun Valley. She did quite well but did not win.

My second year of college I switched schools from Utah State University to the College of Idaho, a Presbyterian school. It was closer to home, so I could go home more often. Not a bad idea. It was a small school with about 500 students, most hailing from within the state of Idaho. One of my favorite teachers was a gentleman who taught Old Testament. I was thinking of going to seminary and becoming a pastor. That all changed when the war came along.

I was visiting at home on the day the war came home for most Americans. My girlfriend and I, along with another couple, were having a snack in a local restaurant. Suddenly the radio program was interrupted by a stern announcement: *Japan had bombed Pearl Harbor.*

Our lives, like many, were changed that day. Many of the students who were old enough immediately joined the service. Nothing was the same. For a long, long time.

I went back to college in January and then decided I needed to be doing something for our country. My mother, bless her heart, called a good friend of ours who was a boss in the electrical department of Kaiser Shipyards in Richmond, California.

This friend of ours, Bud Keating, had been a neighbor about a mile from our farm. He had dropped out of school and taken a job on the construction of the Hoover Dam, on the Colorado River. He had advanced rapidly in the electrical department and become a leader. When the war had come along, Henry Kaiser asked Bud to work in his shipyard. Bud had accepted, and when Mother contacted him, he told her I could have a job with him as an apprentice electrician.

I left college to put in my part for the war effort.

It was our job to keep the electrical welders, lights and other electrical systems operating. It was a huge task When I started we were building a ship a month. Soon it went to one a week. In the short time I was there, I learned a lot about electricity. One of our jobs was to keep the huge cranes working. They ran on 440 volts. If you messed up you could get seriously burned or worse. One time my boss did something that blew him clear across the ship he was working on: a good reminder of the need to be careful around electricity. He ended up black and blue with a beautiful black eye.

I was one among thousands working at Kaiser. I had been blessed to find a room with a wonderful couple who took me in and treated me like a son. They were very warm folks and my stay there was good ***until*** I got a notice from my draft board that the service was really interested in having me join them. The letter started out very friendly, like, "Greetings!" My boss gave me a raise to journeyman electrician. It didn't help. The service had their hands on me.

Before I left for boot camp, my girlfriend and I married.

ꙮ

Now you have read about some of the people and events that helped mold my life and give me the courage and perseverance to come through the terrible times in the war.

I owe a great deal to my parents, who were loving, loyal, strong, determined and patient. They filled my memory with treasure. I loved them with all of my heart while they were alive, and even today my heart is filled as I remember them.

The preacher said it well at my mother's funeral:

"The Father of all mercies must have needed one so vibrant, whose zeal for living blazed trails across the hearts.

Having been born on the American frontier to make her way half way across the continent in a 'prairie schooner' over unmarked roads, she lived to see that wagon track replaced with a super highway. We are told that history repeats itself. Our attention is called to the words of the prophet of God who said, 'And a highway shall be there, and it shall be called the Holy Way.'

It is the lot of some to search out the unknown, to make dreams come true, and it is the lot of most of us to wait until plainly marked thoroughfares have been established. God needs both. They are necessary for His heaven. We doubt not that your beloved Rosa was one of those, whom He challenged to a vibrant faith, to optimism, to ventures of body and spirit. We bless God for giving us this one whose undaunted courage and hope for the future has widened the highway of holiness for us. We know that she has made many of life's difficult situations easier, and He has led the way beyond them."

Finding the Lord was the most important event during this period of my life. How good it was to be able to put all of my burdens at the feet of Jesus. He took them up and set me free. I was young, and He provided guidance. The Bible had not held much interest for me until this time, but now it was revealing Him in ways that had meaning. It was the beginning of a new life for me. Until then, God had always been a distant entity. Now, all of a sudden, He was present within me through the Holy Spirit! I am so glad that He came into my life at such a tender time. His presence made it possible for me to make it through the struggles that were yet to come.

Memories can be great and life sustaining: such were mine!

· 3 ·
THE WAR YEARS

*"For this reason I say to you, do not be anxious for your
life, as to what you shall eat, or what you shall drink;
nor for your body, as to what you shall put on. Is life
not more than food, and the body than clothing?"*
(Matthew 6:26)

That January morning dawned clear and cold. I got my
bags packed and ready to ship out. At the request of
the United States government, I would be joining the ranks
of enlisted personnel at Ft. Douglas, Utah.

When I arrived at the hotel there were several other re-
cruits waiting for the bus to arrive. There were eight of us
departing from our little hometown. We were heading to
who-knows-where, unable to say how many of us would
make the return trip.

It wasn't long until that drab gray Army bus pulled up
and a sharp looking sergeant climbed down the steps. He
looked all of us over with a wry smile, then said in a crisp,
firm voice, "All aboard! We are bound for Ft. Douglas and
will probably arrive in about six hours. There are a few other
stops we must make. So grab your bags and climb aboard."
That was it.

Some of the guys were feeling excited about this new
adventure, but I was not. I was already feeling lonely, and
it took a long time for the doldrums to fade away. Our trip
to Ft. Douglas was not quite as long as the Sergeant said it
would be; we arrived about 2:00 p.m.

Ft. Douglas is one of the oldest forts in the west. It had seen many thousands of troops pass through over the years. As we arrived, the welcoming committee of sergeants lined us up and called out our names, to which we answered, "Here." Where else would we be?

They assigned us to our barracks and said the next step was to get in line and march over to the warehouse to pick up our fine new clothes and bedding. Our GI clothing was all wrinkled and smelled strongly of mothballs.

They asked our sizes and then handed each of us a jacket, pants, shoes, drab underwear, and a long overcoat along with some bedding. Off we went to our barracks to prepare our beds and get ready for inspection.

No one told us how long we would be stationed there. It all depended upon how our tests came out and where we were headed when we left Ft. Douglas.

A few days later I found an iron and an ironing board tucked away in a closet, so I got them out and pressed my clothes. Then another GI came along and asked me to press his clothes. This turned into a slightly profitable enterprise for awhile. I don't have any idea how many things I pressed in the next few days, but my enterprise ended quickly when the First Sergeant came by and observed what I was doing. His eyes shrunk to slight slits and his jaw muscles started to quiver as he looked at me and said in a hoarse raspy voice, "What in the world (he didn't say world) are you doing?" Being quite brave and very ignorant of Army protocol, I told him I was helping my fellow soldiers look sharp in their new uniforms. He didn't think that was such a good idea and immediately told me so. "Put that iron and ironing board away and fall out for inspection." I did.

They ran us through the line and gave us shots for everything imaginable. We were sent to another area to be questioned about what we would like to do in the army. I told them I was a musician and wanted to play in the Army band. That went over like a lead balloon. My next choice was to become an Army Air Force pilot. That must have sounded reasonable, because the next day I was on my way to Nashville, where they ran me through the tests to become a pilot.

It went well until they did the test to check my depth perception. It seemed to mean a lot to these folks that I be able to land a plane correctly, without crashing.

They washed me out of the program immediately. I was shipped to Biloxi, MS, where I learned how to march and stand at attention on the parade field.

Somewhere in this process they decided I would make a good tail gunner, as I was small enough to fit in the tail turret. This meant I would be sent to another station for more training in marching and bivouacking in the woods of Colorado. That was alright with me as I didn't think much of the heat in Biloxi.

They sent me to Denver to learn to be an Armorer. This meant mastering a machine gun, including knowing how to tear down and reassemble a 50-caliber machine gun while blindfolded. Long marches and plenty of work with a machine gun filled my days. One training exercise had us riding on the back of a truck driven in a circle while we shot at clay pigeons as they popped out. We thought that was fun: everyone enjoyed shooting at those little clay birds.

After we learned all there was to learn in Denver we were sent back to Salt Lake City. By then it was winter again, and it was cold! We were living in tents with an old coal-burning stove right in the middle. Someone had to get up at night to stoke the fire.

While we were in Salt Lake our crew was put together:

- Lt. Al Henning, Pilot
- Lt. Walter Escue, Bombardier
- Lt. Fred Lindberg, Navigator
- Flight Officer Kenneth Reed, Copilot
- Sgt. Earl Sullivan, Asst. Radioman
- S/Sgt. Tom Sullivan, Radioman
- S/St. James Smith, Engineer
- Sgt. Wm. Sutton, Asst. Engineer
- Sgt. Robert Otto, Tail Gunner
- Sgt. James Smith, Ball Turret

For further training, they sent us to El Paso, Texas. This was sort of like Biloxi only the heat was dry instead of muggy and hot.

We were assigned an airplane and flew daily missions over the white sands of New Mexico, practice bombing certain targets. Day after day we practiced, our sole purpose being that the bombardier to learn how to find the target and hit it. Sometimes the rest of us would be instructed to fire our machine guns at a target: I think that was just so we would have to break down and clean the machine guns when we got back. It took many missions before the bombardier became accurate and had only near misses. Maybe he should have been a tail gunner.

Our time was not always taken up with flying. We had time to enjoy the luxuries in downtown El Paso, although the only thing I found fulfilling was time spent at several churches I attended. Something in me was saying, "You need to keep in touch with God." That is what I tried to do.

Shortly before we were to be shipped out overseas James Smith, our Engineer, had his girlfriend visit from Texas, and they decided to get married. Al Henning, our pilot, and his wife were living in a small house, and they volunteered to host the wedding. It was a wonderful wedding, and everyone was happy for the bride and groom. There wasn't much time for a honeymoon, but this loving couple managed a short time together.

While training in El Paso we became more than just a crew of guys; we became close knit friends. There were two fellows named Sullivan and two named Smith. None related. I think the enlisted men became closer with each other than the officers, because we lived together and had parties together. I felt good about calling them all my friends.

The officers became our friends too, but there was not the comradeship that there was among the enlisted personnel.

Our time in El Paso came to an end and we had to prepare for our overseas trip. We went to Wichita, Kansas to pick up a new B-24 right off the assembly line.

The first thing that had to be done was to give this young lady a name. That was the prerogative of the pilot, and he named her the **Texarkana Hussy**. His wife was from Texarkana, but she was no hussy.

She was a beautiful, vivacious young lady who livened up all of the events we attended together. All of the enlisted men loved her … from afar.

Our plane was a beauty, and we felt proud to be flying away to war in such a great airplane.

From Wichita we flew to West Palm Beach, Florida, where we stayed overnight. Early the next morning we were off to Trinidad for refueling, and then down South America to Belem, Brazil. Brazil had us wishing we could be stationed there. The food was good, especially the abundant fresh fruit, and Brazil was a long way from the fighting. We stayed overnight there and refueled.

The next morning we were off, over the Atlantic to Africa. This part of the trip was long and monotonous; nothing but water below us. Riding in the back of a big bomber was uncomfortable. Today it's possible to fly across the ocean in just a few hours at five or six hundred miles an hour. Not so back in 1944. Our cruising speed was about three hundred miles an hour. We sat on the floor in the cold space for many, many hours. There is no other way to say it: that was a long journey!

We landed at Dakar, West Africa for refueling then flew on to Algiers for the night. I remember this stop especially well because we awoke in the middle of the night to find an Arab prowling around in our tent. We yelled and scared him away. He was looking for something to sell on the black market. Fortunately, we enlisted men had nothing worth stealing.

From Algiers we flew to our base in Cerignola, Italy where we joined the 459th Bomb Group, 759th Squadron, 304th Bombardment Wing.

Our tents were set up in an olive orchard. This was not a bad setting. The mess hall was not far away and the latrine was even closer. We had it made. The officers were placed somewhere else: they may have been in barracks, though I don't know. Life was good!

That was before we ever went on a mission. Once the missions began, life wasn't so good!

Our First Mission

We rolled out of bed at 4:00 a.m. and headed to the chow hall for a nice breakfast of eggs and pancakes, juice and coffee. Following that fine repast we walked to the briefing room. There, they told us what to bomb and where it was located. A weather report was given.

It was time for our first bombing run. This did not feel like the training flights in El Paso. On all of the flights we had made in El Paso I had gotten sick. Air sickness is no fun! I had felt horrible during all those flights, and I had always come back feeling wobbly and weak. At the time, I had suggested to the commanding officer that it would be better if I could have a desk job someplace. Sounded like a good idea to me, but he hadn't agreed. His reply had been something like, "Get back on that plane. Keep a stiff upper lip. You will get over it." Being a wise airman, I had taken him at his word and continued on the path to throwing up. However, on this flight, our first bombing run, I did not get airsick. Nor did I ever get airsick again. I know it was the tension, and maybe the fear that haunted all of us, that kept my mind so occupied I didn't have time to worry about throwing up.

All our flights were northward, to bombing sights in Italy or somewhere in Germany. On our first trip we were assigned the position of "tail end Charlie." That meant we were the last in the formation and the first to feel the ire of the German fighter pilots. Being the tail gunner, I was the first to see them coming at us like angry bees chasing a camper. Not a pleasant view.

They always meant business. The great desire of the fighter pilots was to knock out a bomber and get an award for downing the enemy.

This first flight for us was truly uneventful. We did not encounter a great number of enemy pilots, and after dropping our bomb load our whole formation came home safely. That was encouraging. We were bombing a target in northern Italy. I remember it well because it was D-Day; the invasion of Normandy.

Until we got into enemy territory our pilot was able to keep us updated on the invasion. We were excited about this invasion. It made us think that the war would be over soon.

This target was close enough that we returned to base, loaded up another bunch of bombs and made another trip to northern Italy. Once again we were able to fly without any loss of planes or crew. This was always a concern.

The policy of our squadron was to give each crew member a jigger of whiskey after coming home from a mission. None of us were drinkers so we decided to put it all in an empty whiskey bottle to drink at a later date. They had told us that after twelve missions we would be granted R&R (rest and relaxation) on the Isle of Capri. This sounded good to all of us, and we began looking forward to it. We had Capri in mind as we saved up our drinking supply for a future date. Trip after trip we put our shots of booze into that bottle. None of us had ever been to Capri, but we had heard good things about the beautiful island and were looking forward to our time there.

Our next bombing run was in southern Germany on a target that was heavily defended by ack-ack guns on the ground and fighter planes in the air. As we approached the target there was so much black material in the air from the 88 millimeter guns that we felt we could walk on it. I received a small wound as a piece of flack came up through the floor of my turret and struck my leg. Fortunately, it was not a serious wound; not worthy of a Purple Heart.

This target was so heavily defended, we did lose a couple of crews. Their planes went down in flames. We didn't know at the time how many had survived or how many had died. Sometime later, this news was reported by the Germans. They wanted us to know, for psychological reasons; to remind us of their power and that we were losing the war. The D-Day invasion had started to turn this whole affair around.

After a mission or two we would get a day off. This was always a welcome thing. Our pilot had brought a little scooter over from the States so he would have transportation to the local town. One day he encountered an Italian driver and crashed into the gutter on his scooter. Fortunately he was only bruised and was able to fly the next day. That was the end of his scooter.

On our next flight we got about half way to our target when engine trouble caused us to abort the mission and return to base. One engine was out and another one was not functioning at full throttle so our pilot decided we had better head home. We were quite a ways north and over the Alps. As we came back, I looked down at those gorgeous mountains and felt like I could just stick my foot out and touch the peaks. We kept losing altitude and by the time we were over the Adriatic Sea we were so low that fishermen were frightened enough to jump out of their boats into the water. We made it home safely!

As time went by, we kept getting deeper and deeper into German territory. We encountered more and more fighter planes as well as increased flak from the ground. The flights became more dangerous each trip. We never knew who would come back. We didn't have any choice in selecting targets. It was, of course, all planned out by officials from some remote headquarters. We were attacking the Germans' oil supplies or armament factories, and they were ferociously defending them. Each time, fewer of our planes came home safely. It was always very sad to come back and find out who had gone down on the mission, despite the fact that many of the men we did not know personally. We were losing so many that they kept adding new crews every week.

It began to appear that the Allies were winning the war, and the Germans became more and more desperate. At the same time, we were getting more and more fighter support on our side. This was very encouraging to all of us.

June 26th dawned bright and early. This was our twelfth mission. The next day we would become eligible for our R&R. Look out Isle of Capri! Every one of our crew was looking forward to time away from the stress of flying on a daily basis. We were all tired and worn down to a nub. You wouldn't believe how stressful the missions had become. Every time we went up several crews did not come back. The question each time was, "Who will be next?" Was it our turn to go crashing down in flames?

Not only were the crews getting stressed, the airplanes were suffering from overwork. Once in a while a crew would come back with their plane crippled and they would crash on landing. These accidents were becoming more common. There was one crew that crashed on takeoff. It seemed more common for crews to abort their flight midway to a target because something was going wrong with the airplane.

Stress! Stress! Stress! I believe the pilots were feeling much more stress than the rest of the crew. We were just riding along. All of the responsibility rested upon the pilots.

Our flights would often be eight to ten hours in length. There we were, up in an airplane without any toilet facilities. What can I say? . When we were in enemy territory we did not dare leave our position. There was no way I could crawl out of my turret for any reason. Life was getting really hard.

Hunger and cold went hand in hand with our need to urinate or go to the toilet. After all, we were human. In training, no one had mentioned the cold. The area from the bomb bay back to the tail turret had two large windows, one on each side, where the waist gunners were located. These were large, open areas for the outside cold to invade. And it did!

At 10,000 feet we had to put on our oxygen masks. Many of our flights were above 20,000 feet. Usually we flew around 26,000 feet. That is the altitude we were headed for on June 26, 1944. Even at that altitude the ground flak could reach up and nail us. None of us complained too much. To whom would we complain? And what good would it do? This was our job. We had to endure.

We usually carried ten 500 pound bombs. That was our bomb bay's capacity. There was a lot of destruction embedded in a load like that We had seen the aftermath of bombed areas in pictures taken by different crews. Usually, almost everything in the area was obliterated; nothing left. Imagine the damage done when fifty or so planes dropped their bombs in an area designated as the target. War is not pretty!!!

Once in a while a bomb might get hung up in the bomb bay and fail to release. Someone had to crawl out on the catwalk and try to release that bomb. That person was in between the two sides of the plane, nothing below him except the ground thousands of feet away. I think this job fell to the engineer. I remember this happening to us only once. The bomb did get released and crashed down somewhere outside the target area. Some of my worst memories came from looking at pictures taken after that raid and seeing how much damage had been done. I felt sorry for the German people who were working or living in that area.

Most of the time our bombardier was accurate in hitting the target. It might have been an oil refinery, a manufacturing facility making components for war, or an area where troops were stationed.

These were days of stress and concern. Every crew flying missions realized how dangerous these flights could be and that any one might be our last. The more flights, the more likely that the one we were beginning could be our last. The Germans were becoming more determined to protect their assets so they continued to reinforce all of their fortifications. The odds of staying safe were getting smaller. All I knew to do was to lean more and more on the Lord for His protection. There was nothing else to do.

· 4 ·
THE LAST FLIGHT

"Do not fear, for I am with you. Do not be anxious.
Look about you, for I am your God. I will strengthen
you, surely I will help you, surely I will uphold you
with My righteous right hand."
(Isaiah 41:10)

As usual, we took off early in the morning. We were assigned to bomb a large oil refinery on the outskirts of Vienna. It was a beautiful summer day, not a cloud in the sky. Our formation rendezvoused over the Adriatic Sea. As the last plane joined the group we headed north with more than fifty planes, escorted by several P-51 fighters. They might have been flown by the Tuskegee Airmen. They often escorted bombers as long as they could, remaining in the air until they had to return to base. As long as they were flying above us, we felt quite safe from the German fighters.

It was a long flight from our base to the target area. The flight was quiet and safe until we got near Vienna. Suddenly, out of the blue above our bombers came a number of German fighter planes with guns a-blazing. It was a hectic few minutes, and our plane was hit. One engine was damaged and set on fire. Then we were in the ack-ack area. There were big guns on the ground blasting away at us. Our plane was hit again by the fighter planes, opening a large hole in the top of the plane and another in the bomb bay. Someone up front said it was big enough for a bathtub. The fire from the engine was getting more serious, yet our pilot managed to get us to the target. We dropped all of our bombs.

Here is a written report from Lt. Herbert Hawkins, a pilot who was flying the same mission, alongside us:

"Almost ten minutes before the bomb run, our formation was hit, and hit hard by more than 50 Me 109s and FW 190s.

They came in close in a series of savage attacks and rockets, blazing away with 22mm cannons.

We saw Henning's plane hit a number of times. There was a large hole extending from the top of the fuselage through the bomb bay doors, and yet the plane flew without a man bailing out.

When the bomb bay doors of Henning's plane were opened on the bomb run, large clouds of smoke and tongues of flame came out. We couldn't figure out how anyone could stand it, but despite the great danger of an explosion at any second, the boys went right on toward the target.

Henning dropped his plane to a lower altitude but maintained his relative formation position to protect the rest of us in event of an explosion, which was momentarily expected.

The crippled plane was still a target of enemy fighters who persisted in their attacks on it, but each man stuck to his post and held off the fighters.

Lt. Henning dropped his bombs on the target and quickly banked away from the target area, leaving the formation.

Now the plane was completely enveloped in smoke and flames, but the pilot still had control.

Not until then, according to the story from the other crews, did Henning give the order to bail out. Seven men came out of the crippled plane in rapid succession, and—just as the last chute blossomed out clear of the plane—there was a puff of fire and smoke and the plane disintegrated in the air.

With the exception of the nose gunner and the copilot, who were killed in this event, the crew was captured and taken prisoners."

And that is what happened to the *Texarkana Hussy* and her crew that day.

All of the crew heard the orders, "Bail out!" And that is exactly what everyone did. Most of the crew dropped out through the bomb bay or the small escape hatch in front of the tail turret. Whitey Smith, the ball turret gunner, had the hardest time getting out. As a result he was severely burned about the face and hands. The others seemed to be relatively free of burns, even though the fire had been raging down the center of the plane. How they escaped severe burns we will never know.

I was the last one to bail out and the only one who had worn a parachute during the flight. All the other crew members had their parachutes lying around someplace in the plane. They had to find them, immediately fasten them on and then bail out. My parachute was on, under my flak vest. The plan was to take the vest off first, then jump and pull the parachute. It didn't work that way!

The fire was raging down the center of the plane with such fury that I did not have time to do anything except crawl to the escape hatch and jump. As I hit the slip stream of the plane, I started somersaulting, at the same time trying to grab the fasteners of my flak vest to get free of it. The vest fit over my head like an apron and came down below my bottom, where the fasteners were secured around my legs. After tumbling for what seemed like forever, I got the fasteners loose, pulled the vest over the top of my head and dropped it. Immediately I pulled the cord on my parachute and it blossomed out. What a relief!

People have asked me whether I was scared during all of this. My answer has always been, "No. I didn't have time to be scared." When things happen as fast as they did then, there is no time for fear to enter. We were so busy trying to escape that fear never made itself present to our minds.

With my chute open, I looked out in the direction of the plane and saw it disintegrate in mid air.

Within a few minutes I was hanging in a tree. Freeing myself from the parachute I dropped to the ground and attempted to hide in some bushes. That didn't work. There were people all around. They were local folks with clubs and pitchforks, and maybe a gun or two. There were no German soldiers to be seen. Some of these folks were small children. One gentleman took me by the arm and helped me up. This gentleman escorted me down the hill towards the local jail.

While walking down the trail, my face began to give me pain. I was badly burned, but did not know the extent. When we came to a small puddle of water, I stopped to see if I could catch my reflection. I couldn't.

As I walked into the jail, I saw six other members of our crew. Six plus me made seven. Where were the other three? None of us knew.

Somehow we got from that little jail to a hospital in the city of Graz, Austria, some forty-five minutes away. Whitey was suffering from the worst burns, my burns being the next in severity. We stayed in this hospital several days. They treated us by applying sulfa powder to our wounds. As the wounds healed, the hospital staff carefully (as careful as possible) pealed off the crusty scabs. I don't remember how many days we were hospitalized, but I do remember that they took good care of us.

The quick healing that took place from my severely burned face was a miracle. There was no other way to put it. God was still taking care of me and there was nothing else that I could do than to trust Him for all things. He is the One who saved my life! I came through without any serious scarring; Whitey carried his scars to his grave, more than fifty years later.

When we were pretty well healed they took us out of this hospital to the city of Salzburg, where we were put into solitary confinement. This was a lonely time. We never knew what was going on and never saw each other. At times they would come after one us to be taken before a German officer for interrogation. He was a very polite man who spoke perfect English. As we entered his office he arose and offered a cigarette or cup of coffee.

Then he began the inquisition, asking where we were based, how many missions we had been on, who was the commanding officer, and on and on. None of us gave him any information that he didn't already have: he told us where we were stationed, how many planes there were and the name of our commanding officer. The Germans knew all about our operation.

Our solitary cells were about eight feet long and six feet wide. There was a small window near the ceiling, too high to reach. If we needed to use the toilet we had to pull a little lever that would cause a little arm to stick out into the hallway, where the guards could observe it and come to escort each one of us. There was a single bed fastened to the wall, holding a thin mattress and a single blanket. Fortunately for us it was June, and the weather was warm.

I never saw the rest of the crew in this place. Nor did I see them after we were moved to Stalag Luft IV (for the enlisted men). (The officers were also moved, probably to Stalag Luft 1.)

It was only long after the war that I once again met three of my crew mates. One year, Lt. Henning and his wife, Jane, drove from their home in Iowa and visited us in Idaho. He had become a Captain, and he stayed in the service for several more years. After he retired, he bought a farm in Iowa and lived there until he passed away. His son, Mike, now lives and works on the farm. Mike came to visit us in Washington state one year, and we call each other just to keep in touch.

A few years later I went to see Jim Smith, the Engineer, in Texas, but he passed away before I arrived. I did get to visit with his wife and son, Dan.

Several years later, Tom Sullivan called me from Long Island, NY. He was coming to Boise, Idaho for a POW Reunion and asked if my wife and I could meet him and his wife there. We did and had a great few days together. A few years later Tom died. Mary, his widow, came for a visit a few years ago. My wife and I keep in touch with Mary via the internet.

We kept in touch with Whitey Smith, at least at Christmas time, until he passed away a few years ago. We still keep in contact with his widow.

I never heard from any of the other officers or Bill Sutton. Bill was not captured with the rest of us. He escaped for a couple of weeks and then was caught. That is all I know about him. I tried all the ways possible to locate him but always came up blank. As far as I know, I am the lone survivor of the *Texarkana Hussy.*

After our interrogation was completed we were loaded into boxcars and moved north, where we ended up in Stalag Luft IV. This was a miserable trip. There were so many prisoners of war that there was standing room only in our boxcar. The journey took several days. Our boxcar became a cesspool of urine and fecal waste. It was awful, to say the least. Once in a while the train would stop, and they would let us out for a short while under the watchful eyes of a number of German guards. Sometimes the train would pull off on a siding to allow other trains to use the tracks. Those trains were usually carrying war supplies to the front lines. One day the bombers from England came to bomb a train, and we were very near that site. Everyone thought we were going to be blown into tiny pieces. We did feel the impact of those bombs as they shook the whole area around us, but we were not hit. I don't know how long this train ride was. I do know it wasn't anything I would like to repeat.

By the time we got to our destination, we were all exhausted and grumpy. We were greeted at the train station by a number of German guards and guard dogs, mostly German Shepherds. Imagine that! We were lined up for the two mile walk to Stalag Luft IV, and the guards let us know they wouldn't stand for any funny stuff. They were quite willing to use the bayonet, and the dogs were always available to chew on men who got out of line or lagged behind. Those dogs meant business. It was not a friendly meeting!

What kind of life were we going to have behind barbed wire? None of us knew what to expect. The march was an indication that things would not go well.

All I could do was to trust in the Lord for protection, survival and encouragement. Now, as I look back, it is clear to me that He provided all of this. The more I believed in God and trusted Him the more it became evident that He was watching over me.

LIFE AS A KREIGIE

"Do not be anxious saying, 'What shall we eat?' or 'With
what shall we clothe ourselves?' for our Heavenly Father
knows that you need all these things."
(Matthew 6:31-32b)

Stalag Luft IV, located near the Baltic Sea, was a camp opened to Americans on May 12, 1944. The camp was one-quarter complete when the first prisoners ("kreigie" in German) arrived. The capacity was 6,400 POW's. By January 1945 there were 10,000 or more. Located in the center of a clearing in a pine forest, the camp was divided into five compounds, or lagers ABCD and the vorlager. The vorlager housed the German personnel barracks and the infirmary, food warehouse (where the Red Cross parcels were stored), clothing and a hospital.

The POW area had dormitory-type barracks, with ten sleeping rooms designed for sixteen POW's per room. That was the plan, but it became necessary to put twenty-four men in each room and use three-tiered bunks. Even then some of the men had to sleep on the floor. Each room had a small coal stove for heat, only used part of the day (mostly at night before lights out). POW's were locked in their barracks from 4:00 p.m. until 7:00 a.m.

Each lager had two open-air latrines with two twenty-holers back to back with urinals. The toilet pits were pumped out by the Russian prisoners, and the waste was spread on the fields. They had a wagon which was made for this purpose. It had a huge round tank fitted with a suction pump that worked as a piston. They had some type of firing mechanism they could light, and it would explode and suck everything from the pit into the tank. Then it was spread on the fields outside of the compound.

Each lager had two outside wells with pumps to provide water for drinking and washing. The water was tested and found to be potable. There were no cases of typhoid or cholera.

At first there were no facilities for bathing or delousing, and there were parasites such as fleas, lice and bedbugs.

Food included a daily ration of bread made of 50% bruised rye grain, 20% sliced sugar beets, 20% tree flour (sawdust) and 10% minced leaves or straw. Prisoners were served boiled potatoes and some soup mixture of potato, turnip, carrot, dehydrated sauerkraut, rutabaga, kohlrabi and some meat (mostly horse meat). Several times a week the prisoners were served cooked barley and millet. The average weight loss of the prisoners was 15 to 20 pounds before the forced march began in February 1945.

Red Cross parcels were stored in a warehouse and handed out at the commanding officer's pleasure. If there were any mix ups, fights, or acts of insubordination he would withhold or halve a parcel. Sometimes weeks would go by without Red Cross parcels. The Red Cross parcels contained dried milk, cocoa, cigarettes, candy bars, cheese, crackers, jelly, various types of dried meat and maybe cereal, like oatmeal. It wasn't glamorous food, but to the POW's it was a little bit of home.

In the medical area there was no dental clinic and the hospital had just over 100 beds. There was one bathtub in the hospital and no bed sheets. There were no facilities for major surgery and no X-ray equipment. Sick call was from 10:30 to 12:00 each day, and each lager had a makeshift dispensary. Here is a list of diseases that occurred while in this *stalag.* Upper respiratory, tonsillitis, diarrhea, skin diseases, diphtheria, jaundice, tuberculosis, meningitis, hemorrhoids, arthritis and 15-20% with war wounds.

On July 17, 18, 19 and August 5, 6, 1944 Americans and British were treated for bayonet wounds, dog bites, clubbed areas while they were forced to run from the railroad station to the camp (a distance of two miles). One prisoner was bayoneted and his medical record indicated "sun stroke," because he had been given a tetanus shot. No prisoners died from this ordeal, but it was estimated that over 100 prisoners were treated for wounds and dog bites and one POW had over sixty wounds and dog bites. These were POW's that were transferred from another Stalag Luft.

It wasn't all fun and games. Most days were filled with monotony. Some people would walk the perimeter of the compound. Others would sit around and talk. I belonged to a small group that held daily Bible studies. One of our prisoners was a Baptist minister, and he led our studies. This was the highlight of our day. We did a lot of praying, and I know it helped each of us keep hope. We had faith that Jesus was watching out for us. This was particularly helpful while we were on the long march near the end of the war. I found my strength in believing God was in charge, and knowing I was one of his children. .

There were people in our compound who were talented in acting and music. At Christmas time, December 1944, a musical theatre program was staged. We had musical instruments that the Red Cross had made available. It was a time of enjoyment and laughter with everybody singing, "We'll be Home for Christmas." Didn't happen! It was a highlight of the year and really helped break up the boredom.

Everyone looked forward to mail call. We were allowed mail and to write two letters a month. Most of us didn't get much mail, but if one of our buddies received a food package from home it was shared by all. There was a real feeling of being a buddy.

One of my close friends was a Jewish fellow from Brooklyn who spoke fluent German. I got to know him really well. He would talk to the guards and work out trades, exchanging cigarettes or a candy bar for a favor from them. It worked out quite well for us since neither he nor I smoked. We willingly exchanged cigarettes for extra food.

There was one guard who could speak English. We found out that he had moved to the United States very early in the Nazi regime. He came back in the late 1930s to visit his family and they put him in the army. He was too old to be on the front lines so they had sent him to take care of the POW's at Stalag Luft IV. He was a very nice fellow and we got to know him a little bit. He had to be very careful because they did not allow fraternizing with the prisoners.

Another guard was a Lithuanian who was forced into the army. He had been wounded and lost an eye. He wore a patch over this eye. He could speak English, but he was not too friendly.

There were other guards in our compound who didn't like us much but none like "Big Stoop." Stationed in one of the other compounds, he was big and mean. He enjoyed hitting prisoners. Rumor had it that with one punch he could put you out for a week. No one dared cross him. He died during the long march. It was rumored that some of the American prisoners killed him along the way. Here is the story as recorded in *The Last Escape,* by John Nichol and Tony Rennell:

"For one dead German, however, there would be no pity or remorse, Big Stoop, the giant from Stalag Luft IV at Gross Tychow came all the way with the prisoners to Moosburg. He could not have known how hated he was and how many men had sworn to get even with him. There are various accounts of his death. None is pleasant. One prisoner said he saw two prisoners carrying his head in a bushel basket. Another account said he was spread-eagled across a road with a pick axe in his head. His evil actions caught up to him."

Time in a POW camp was tiresome, lonely, and sometimes agonizing. We never knew what was going to happen to us. No one had any idea whether we would make it home. There was the possibility that Hitler would have all POW's put to death. This threat came down through the grapevine, and it hung over our heads as a possibility.

Most of our days were pretty routine. Up by 7:00 to stand outside in formation for a body count. Every morning and evening this was the story. We would line up and a guard would attempt to count us. Then someone might move to another group and the count would be off, so another count was ordered. The guards never caught on to what we were doing; just something to confuse and annoy our guards.

Each compound had an American enlisted man who acted as our contact with the Commandant. He would take our complaints and problems to the officers on a daily basis.

Usually, nothing would come of this, but at least the Germans knew how we were feeling and the needs we wanted them to meet. For instance, we may not have received a Red Cross parcel for a week or so. This would be taken to the Commandant and he would consider the problem. The next week we might get a half order. It all depended upon how we were doing at being obedient and not causing problems. It didn't take much for them to withhold these parcels. We always thought the Germans were eating more of them than the prisoners.

Every noon someone from each barracks would take a bucket or two to the kitchen, and the cooks would fill it up with whatever we were having that day. Then in the evening they would repeat this routine. Most of the food we received was pretty watered down and not very healthy or fulfilling. One time the cooks had an idea that if all the prisoners would give them the raisins that came in the Red Cross parcels they would put them into one of the large cooker pots in the kitchen and make some "home brew." Every barracks complied with enthusiasm. About the time the brew was ready to dispense to the different barracks, the Germans got word of what was happening. When the cooks got word that the Germans were going to put a stop to this, they rushed buckets full of the brew to each barracks. We all had a jolly time that evening, and the Germans didn't catch anyone.

Most of the guards were older men who had served in the front lines somewhere and now were allowed to have a less demanding job. And most of those in our compound were pretty good guys. We had the feeling that their hearts were not always in their jobs and that is why we got along quite well with them. The fact that some of the prisoners could converse in German helped. The prisoners were always trying to find some type of activity to keep occupied. Whether it was harassing the guards or playing some kind of games, we were seeking ways to keep busy and make time go by a little faster.

One day a German fighter plane flew over the camp with the plane seeming to be in trouble. As we looked upward and saw that it was losing power, we all said a prayer in unison saying, "Crash." I don't know whether this was an answer to prayer or not, but a few minutes later we heard a loud explosion and then a huge plume of smoke arose beyond the forest. We never heard anything about it

Occasionally the guards would come through the barracks to check on contraband or the possibility of someone having a short wave radio. There were people in each compound who knew enough to build a radio out of a few parts. Fortunately it was possible to bribe a guard now and then to help get these supplies smuggled in. These guards would almost destroy our rooms as they tore our beds apart, tossing the bedding and mattresses on the floor and then pouring our Red Cross parcels out upon them. This included honey, jelly, and powdered milk. It was a very messy affair, which we had to clean up. While all of this was going on inside the barracks, we had to stand in formation on the parade area, come rain, snow or cold. After they had destroyed or messed up everything to the best of their abilities, we were allowed back inside to clean it up. You can imagine the loud griping that this produced as we took everything outside and washed it down.

Life wasn't always easy! I was still learning to trust in the Lord.

There were rules and regulations that it was best to obey. Ten feet inside the large fence that surrounded the camp a wire ran along a line of posts, to prevent anyone from attempting an escape. If a prisoner went beyond this wire he was to be immediately shot from one of the guard towers. This was truly *verboten*. One prisoner tried it and was shot dead. At night our barracks were locked down and all lights turned off. One night a prisoner went berserk and jumped through a window. He was shot dead.

It was nearly a year since I had come to this camp when the Russians decided to move west from their occupation of Poland. We were fairly close to that area. Then one day we could hear the guns of the Russians. Their cannons were blasting away at the German forces, which were retreating at a rapid pace. One morning we awoke, and our guards told us to pack up our goods and be prepared to leave. They planned on marching us a few days to the west, out of the reach of the Russians. This didn't sound too bad, so we tried to pack everything we could carry. It was early February and very, very cold and miserable weather. Each one of us put on all the clothes we had, filled our pockets with as much food as we could and tried to save any mementos we had accumulated. With our one blanket we were ready to march.

· 6 ·
THE LONG MARCH

*"Even though I walk through the valley of the
shadow of death, I fear no evil, for Thou art with
me; Thy rod and thy staff comfort me. "*
(Psalm 23)

The Germans were evacuating the whole camp in groups of several hundred men at a time, over a period of several days. There were 10,000 prisoners that had to be sent someplace. These men were marched off in different directions to end up at some other Stalag farther to the west. We did not know our destination as we started out, nor did we learn it throughout the march. We just took off. Sometimes we wondered whether the officers and guards had any idea where we were going, as day after day we wandered around the countryside.

In the beginning we were assured it would only be for a few days, so we were able to walk briskly, expecting that there would be another camp for us to move into. After a few days it became evident that they were going to keep us marching for a long period of time. My life had never been one of luxury, but here I was entering a path in a dark wood. Imagine us on a blind path, having to follow the men who imprisoned us.

Fortunately, I had a light inside. Sometimes I could not see it, but God tended that light for many days and nights.

Things were pretty good at the beginning of the march, as we had a few goodies from our Red Cross parcels to keep us going. At night they tried to find a farm that had a large barn where we could sleep. Some nights we slept out in the fields with only our one blanket and our heavy overcoat to keep us as warm as possible. It was not possible, and when we were forced to sleep in a field there was no food to serve us. When we stayed in a barn the farmer usually had a large cooking vat used to boil potatoes for their cows. The guards would load the vat with spuds and boil them up until tender, then give them to us to eat. No salt and pepper, no butter, no nothing! If the Germans had any Red Cross parcels in the wagons that attended us, then we might share these. Sometimes we would have that wonderful sawdust bread. A loaf of that bread, which in our country would weigh one pound, weighed nearer two pounds. It was heavy and thick, but we learned to love it, because it was, at least, filling. There was no butter or peanut butter or jelly to put on the bread, just dry bread. Day after day this was our routine.

This was the winter of the Battle of the Bulge, one of the coldest and snowiest winters in history. Many soldiers died from the cold while serving in the front lines, and so it was with our POW's marching through the snow and cold day after day. There might be a man walking alongside of you and suddenly he wasn't there anymore. He had collapsed and fallen by the side of the road or into the field. This happened to several of my friends. Some were fortunate enough to be picked up by the guards and delivered to someplace that would care for them. Others froze to death, or died in the fields from pneumonia or dysentery. Frozen feet and hands were very common. To say the least, it was hell!

After the war we were told that about twenty five percent of the prisoners on this march died. Why were others spared to live? I don't know. All I know is that God was watching over me. He gave me the strength and courage to keep on keeping on. I owe my life to Him.

Day after day and night after night we struggled and shivered to keep alive. No one was ever warm.

One night while we were sleeping in a barn I was struck by dysentery. I had to run for my life to get out of the barn and relieve myself. It wasn't easy. I was sleeping in the middle of a hundred other guys and had to crawl over them in the best way I could. Unfortunately I didn't make it. I filled my underwear. Standing out in the middle of a snow-covered field I took off my pants and long johns. I had to throw my underwear away, and there weren't any spares. I pulled my pants on and climbed over the sleepers back to my spot. Without long underwear I was colder than ever. How I missed them!

It turned out we were about halfway to our destination. There were still many days and nights to fight off the cold. I remember thinking "OH GOD, HOW MUCH LONGER? I don't think I can make it Lord." Then a small voice from within said, "Have courage, my son, I am with you."

At that time God was like my family. As an infant, when I would turn blue a family member would rush me outside to help me breathe, assuring me on some level that they wanted me to live. There was no doubt in my being that living is what I was meant to do. It's just that, once again, I could not do it without someone to carry me.

When we would wake after a restless night on the ground or the floor of a cold barn, our joints didn't want to cooperate or move as we expected. Our frostbitten feet refused to function in a normal manner. Our hands were stiff and tender to the touch. Nothing seemed to want to go another day; every cell in our bodies cried out, "Enough is enough."

This was the period when many of the men just gave up. They simply refused to go another step. Time had run out for them. Several were left in barns or in the fields, hoping that a German wagon would come along. It was a possibility for some, if there was room on one of the wagons. Others were just left there, and no one knew what became of them.

March arrived. We had been walking for a month; thirty long, dreary, dreadful, frozen days. No one wanted to go another step.

Eventually the weather began to warm a degree or two per day. The snow stopped falling, and the air became a bit warmer. We who were still able to walk were feeling better and encouraged, not by our guards, but by the warmth. The frozen ground began to thaw and became a muddy mess. One day we woke up to rain. This complicated our walk as the mud stuck to our boots in great gobs. Each step became more laborious, as we slipped and slid this way and that. No one told us, because no one knew, that it was April.

Tender little flowers were beginning to push up through the ground and the air began to warm. What a blessing! But the march wasn't over yet. There were a number of days left. Finally we arrived at a camp. It had been seventy days of traveling for us, and we were exhausted.

Everyone thought this was the end. Not so! The camp was already full to overflowing with prisoners. A group of our people could stay. The rest of us would have to move on. I was in the "move on" group.

Off we went to find another place to stay. We wandered around for several days, staying in barns without any information about our destination. After a number of days we returned to the camp, where room was finally made available. This was a camp of British POW's. They welcomed us with open arms and a cup of tea. Soon we learned how to boil tea in a tin can.

Then one day we awakened and all of the guards were gone. They knew the Allies were fast approaching and they didn't want to be caught. We didn't know anything. But, since the guards were gone we opened the gates and walked down the road to where there was a large warehouse. Since no one was around we thought it would be a good idea to see what was inside. We pried open the door and were surprised to see it filled with Red Cross cartons. Right off, we opened one and proceeded to enjoy some good American food.

We walked back to the compound wondering what was happening. As we were discussing the opportunity of escaping, we heard the banging and rattling of tanks approaching. We thought they were Americans, but it turned out to be a British tank unit that set us free.

We were free at last!

What could we do with this freedom? Finally some American soldiers arrived, and we were escorted to another place, and eventually to an Army base in Belgium. There they cleaned us up. First we were deloused and then, for the first time in months, we were able to take a hot shower, have a shave and brush our teeth. Is it possible to imagine yourself in a predicament where you did not have a shower, a chance to brush your teeth or use toilet paper for seventy days?

None of us had known how hard life was going to be during the march. We had no idea we were being sent on a death march. And all I knew afterwards was that God had provided for me each day of the march. He kept me going, when I was ready to quit. Giving thanks was not much payment to God for all He was doing, but it was all I had to offer, and I poured out my thanks every day. He was the one Who gave me the energy, the determination, and the fortitude to plod on. Thank you Lord for the encouragement provided. It saved my life.

What a joyous feeling to be clean! We were overwhelmed. We sat down to a dinner with more food than we had seen in a year. We dove in and had ourselves a feast, ending with a large dish of ice cream.

Suddenly, we were all rushing to get outside where we immediately threw up everything we had just eaten. Our stomachs could not tolerate all of the food. Fortunately, it only took a day or so to adjust. We began eating normal Army food.

Our next stop was Camp Lucky Strike. This was a tent village not too far from Paris, and the starting point of our trip home. Lucky Strike was an embarkation point where we would wait until a ship was available to take us across the Atlantic Ocean to the United States of America: our destination.

We didn't know how long we would be here. Some of the fellows decided to go into Paris. I decided to stay in camp in case my name was called to move out. It didn't get called that day, and I missed the chance to visit Paris. Home sounded better to me.

It wasn't long until a ship was available at Le Havre. We sailed to Southampton, England and then on to New York. It was an uneventful trip except for my sea sickness. After a day or so I adjusted and was able to join the other men in the mess hall.

The greatest sight of all was the Statue of Liberty. As we pulled into the harbor, I thought I knew how the early immigrants felt as they arrived in America. Free at last!

*High School
Graduation
1940*

*Training Graduation
1944*

*above: B-24 Bomber "Liberation Over the Alps"
   by Nicolas Trudgian. Used by permission of the artist.*

below: Proud American Veteran, June 2004

above and opposite: Crew of the Texarcana Hussy, 1944

Standing L to R:
2nd Lt. Albert Henning, Pilot;
2nd Lt. Walter Escue, Bombardier;
2nd Lt. Fred Lindberg, Navigator;
Flight Officer Kenneth Reed, Copilot (KIA).

Sitting L to R:
Sgt. E.E. Sullivan, Asst. Radioman (KIA);
S/Sgt. Thomas Sullivan, Radioman;
S/Sgt. James Smith, Engineer
Sgt. William Sutton, Asst. Engineer
Sgt. Robert Otto, Armorer
Sgt. Warren Smith, Gunner

above: Tail section of the Texarkana Hussy, late summer 1944

Wreckage typically would be removed by locals for use in construction. This photo provided by Josef Schutzenhofer, who noted, "It took [the locals] awhile to remove the remaining section."

below and lower right: Stalag Luft IV
used by permission courtesy of
B-24 Net
www.b24.net/pow/rose/photos.html

above: Red Cross parcel
below: Stalag Luft IV
both photos used by permission courtesy of B-24 Net
www.b24.net/pow/rose/photos.html

above and next page: The Long March
both photos used by permission courtesy of B-24 Net

· 7 ·
HOME AT LAST

*"Do not lay up for yourself treasures upon earth
where moth and rust destroy, and where thieves
break in and steal. For where your treasure is. There
will be your heart also."
(Matthew 5:19,21)*

After a few days at Fort Kilmer I boarded a train for the cross country trip back to Idaho. My folks greeted me with hugs and tears. It was an exceptionally warm meeting, but where was my wife?

A little while later she came to see me. She had been working. Hers was not the warm and loving welcome that I had anticipated. After a year in a POW camp and nothing on my mind except how life would be when I got home, this was an unpleasant surprise. My wife said she wanted a divorce. Why? I didn't understand. Had I done something wrong? No that wasn't it at all. She had found someone else to be with during my time away. Maybe she thought I would never come home. I don't know what she thought.

It was a terrible blow to me. She got the divorce, and I decided to enjoy life by going to the bars and drinking. One of my good buddies had come home from the Navy, so he and I tried drinking all of the booze in our little hometown. He never gave it up and died an alcoholic.

The Army was good to all of us POW's and gave us a forty-five day leave. I enjoyed this time with my good friends and my drinking buddies.

The Army sent me to California for reassignment. I was stationed in a hotel on the beach at Santa Monica. This was tough duty! We had to answer roll call early each morning, but if our name wasn't on the list to be shipped out we had the day free to do whatever we wanted. I was there when the Japanese surrendered, and Hollywood came alive!

It took about two weeks for me to be reassigned. They asked me what kind of a job I wanted and where I wanted to be stationed. My choice was to be a truck driver and to be sent to Gowen Field, Boise, Idaho. Both of these wishes were approved, and off to Boise I went.

My assignment was to pick up baggage at the downtown train depot and deliver it to the warehouse. My boss was a ci- vilian. He and I got along just fine. When the weekend would come around I would ask him if I could get off early to go home. He always said yes if there wasn't any baggage to pick up. I would get out on the highway, stick up my thumb and immediately get a ride. Anyone in a uniform in those days was respected and honored. It was easy to get 100 miles to my hometown and then back on a Sunday afternoon.

During the few months I was stationed at Gowen Field, life was good. I almost enjoyed the Army. When my dis- charge papers came up they offered me a job as a recruiter with a raise in grade. I would have been a Tech Sergeant. My answer was, "No, thanks." I wanted to return to the civilian life. And so I did.

I lived with my folks, in town, and worked on the farm just a mile out of town.

Only a few months after I had returned home from the service I thought it would be fun to learn to ski. Sun Valley was only an hour's drive from our home. At that time it was operated by the Navy, to rehabilitate injured sailors. I was able to buy secondhand skis from the Navy, and thus began my skiing time.

The skis we had were very long. Ski experts had determined that skis should be as tall as your reach with your arm fully-extended above your head. That made them long and awkward, but they were the best available at the time. I started on the bunny hill, and gradually the hills got higher and steeper. The first time I went up on Baldy Mountain with my friends it seemed like an impossibility to get to the bottom. That mountain was so steep, and it was a long way back down to the lift! We managed to get down with a number of falls in the snow, usually head first. But Baldy Mountain became my favorite ski place for many reasons, including the charm of boyhood memories: it was one of the mountain areas where my dad used to run sheep.

A good looking girl lived across the street from my parents. She knew about my situation and thought she could help me out by lining me up with a blind date. I was not too anxious to date again, but she and her husband were persistent. They thought it would be nice if I would go out with them and this new girl.

And that is the way it happened. When we went out, Mary Ann and I found we had much in common. We fell in love and were married three months later. We had a simple wedding with family and a few friends.

We celebrated our honeymoon in Ketchum, Idaho, where Mary Ann's mom owned a little, old house. Ketchum is the little town where Sun Valley was built. Ketchum had a large swimming pool heated by natural hot water from a spring up in Warm Springs valley. Most of the old homes in Ketchum were heated by this water. People came from all over to swim in this pool. During our honeymoon in Ketchum, Mary Ann went to the grocery store and saw Clark Gable buying groceries. She couldn't wait to get home and tell me about this sighting. She was very excited!

Over the years, Mary Ann and I saw many celebrities visiting Ketchum and Sun Valley. Bing Crosby and Gary Cooper used to hang out at Sun Valley in the fall, during pheasant hunting season, and Mary Ann saw them in downtown Ketchum. She should have carried a tablet with her to get autographs from all those stars. And they were stars in those days! Once we saw Dick Powell and June Allyson, his wife. They were sitting at an outdoor table drinking coffee and as we walked by she said, "Dickie, won't you tie my shoes?" His reply was, "Tie them yourself." Isn't it strange the things that stick in our minds? One time, many years later, I was skiing down Baldy Mountain and standing along the way chatting with a group of people was Clint Eastwood. I was going many miles an hour when one of the fellows I was with said, "Look, there is Clint Eastwood." About that time I ran right over the back of Clint's skis. I thought, "Oh my gosh what have I done?" I expected him to pick up his ski poles, take off after me, and beat me. He didn't even know what I had done and his skis were not scarred or scraped. It was all in my mind.

When Mary Ann and I returned from our honeymoon, we were able to move into my folks' home while they were in Arizona for the winter. Life was good again! In 2009, we celebrated our 63rd year in a happy marriage. God is good! He blessed me. Again!

Mary Ann was working as a clerk in the county office of the Auditor, Recorder and County Clerk. One day, while I was working with my dad on the farm, the chairman of the county Republican party stopped by for a chat. His whole purpose was to ask me if I would like to run for a county office. I had no plans to do such a thing but after talking it over with my dad it seemed like a good idea. Here is where I went wrong. I didn't talk to my wife about it. Right there and then we signed the papers, and the Chairman took them in to file in the very office where my wife worked. When her boss saw papers stating that I was going to run against her she immediately fired my wife. That night when I, in my simple bliss came home, Mary Ann was more than slightly irritated. She had been fired, and it was my fault. *We had a talk!*

Things worked out and we went on the campaign trail. It was a lot of fun meeting with people in all of the little towns in our county. Once I was asked to speak on the radio. We had pamphlets printed and passed out everywhere we could. One of our close friends had a dog named Snorky, a Water Spaniel. He was a wanderer and covered the whole town. Everyone knew Snorky. We made a sign and put it on him so everyone could read it: This is what it said: "If I were a man, I would vote for Otto." This little gimmick drew a lot of attention.

Election night came and we all sat around waiting for the results. I was anxious about the outcome, and it was a nail biting evening. Finally, the news came through. We had won!!! I was officially the County Auditor, Recorder and Clerk of the District Court.

What did I know about running a county office? Nothing! Fortunately, I had a competent assistant in the office.

I depended upon her. She stayed on for a few months and taught me all I needed to know about the workings of this office. She was a very pleasant and capable teacher.

My best friend in the courthouse turned out to be the Prosecuting Attorney. We often went to the local drugstore to have a milkshake at the soda fountain, and he was most helpful. At the time, political parties wanted to reward veterans who returned home, and another friend got elected to the Sheriff's Office. The three of us worked together and managed to keep our offices properly functioning.

Mary Ann and I had been living in a very small duplex. It was a tiny, one bedroom place with a very small living room and an even smaller kitchen. In those early years we didn't mind, because we were so in love that it was enough just to be together. The folks next door to us were friends. The husband had been a classmate of Mary Ann's in high school and his wife worked for me in the courthouse. The walls were so thin that we could have conversations right through them! It was a great place for newlyweds, but not for entertaining.

Mary Ann and I moved into a small home on five acres. It had a barn, so I could have a horse and that made me happy. I was working in the courthouse and helping run my Dad's farm, which was just a mile out of town. I could jump on my horse and ride out there in a few minutes to do some work. We rented a forty acre farm nearby that had a small peach orchard. These years were very pleasant. We had many good friends, and we were able to spend time with both friends and family. Life was good.

Running the county office turned out to be a valuable experience for me, and I enjoyed my time there. I was elected for a four year term, but after two years I felt like I was spinning my wheels, so I resigned my position. The County Commissioners found someone to take over.

My father and I bought a 100-acre farm with a large, new barn and a new house. Mary Ann and I had our first child, a daughter, while living there. The farm was a delightful place with a clear stream winding through the corral where we kept our cattle.

I tried to make a farm wife out of Mary Ann. She had grown up in town and never lived on a farm, except when her father was in charge of a state game farm that raised pheasants. I expected too much of her. She had to learn to cook for four or five workers at times. It was a challenge she rose to and did well. I also wanted her to help with driving the tractor and working in the fields alongside of me. This was a little too much. She never really learned to drive the tractor without getting everything all tangled up. "Maybe," I thought, "she really wasn't cut out to be a farmer's wife."

VETERINARY MEDICINE

"A good man is concerned for the welfare of his animals."
(Proverbs 12:10, The Living Bible)

One day, a few years later, I had our veterinarian out to treat one of the cows. While he was working away, we were busy visiting. He thought I ought to become a veterinarian, and in the course of conversation he told me the best school to attend was Colorado State University in Ft. Collins. This sounded like a good idea, but I needed a few more college credits to even apply to vet school.

I talked this over with my Dad, and he thought it was a good idea as farming was becoming more expensive and less profitable each year. We sold the farm. The profit I made was to go towards my education. Mary Ann and I bought a trailer to live in and moved to Colorado. We found a student trailer park near the school and quickly became friends with our neighbors. One was a senior in vet school, and he helped me line up my schedule. They had a daughter about the same age as ours. We all became close friends and still keep in contact more than fifty years later.

When I finished that year of school I had enough credits to apply to vet school. Unbeknownst to me, it was very difficult to get into vet school. Only one in ten applicants were accepted across the whole country, as there were only a few schools and many people wanted to become veterinarians. No one had told me this, and I simply hadn't realized it. This seemed like an insurmountable obstacle, but I had to try. Fortunately for me, I had made good grades this last year.

I made out applications for the Veterinary College at Colorado State and also at Washington State College. I sent them to the schools and awaited a reply. The way it worked was like this: you applied and waited and hoped for an interview. If they interviewed you then you waited to find out what the results would be. Accepted? Rejected?

In only a few weeks I got an answer from Washington State College. They had accepted me, without an interview. Unheard of! Some One must have been looking out for me.

A little while later I was scheduled for an interview at Colorado State. This gave us hope that we might be able to stay in Colorado: we had come to love the mountains, the little town of Ft. Collins and the friends we had made.

The day for my interview arrived. The Dean asked me if I had been in contact with other schools, and if so what had been the results. I told him that I had been accepted at Washington State College. He then told me that they would not consider me, as it would deprive someone else of the chance to apply. This ended our time in Colorado.

The next move was back home to Idaho. We sold our little twenty-six foot trailer and moved into college housing at Washington State University. Thus we entered a new phase of our lives.

I loved going to vet school, even though I was the oldest in my class. It was tough. The courses were hard and the hours were long. We were in school six days a week. I studied hard and tried to have time with the family, but it was a struggle. It took hours every night to study.

We needed some financial help so I applied for a job in the Anatomy Department at the vet school. The pay was

$1.00 an hour. The most important part of this job was to embalm all of the animals used in the anatomy classes.

We had to embalm dogs, cats, cattle, sheep and horses. The arteries were injected with a red dye and the veins with a blue dye to make it easier for the students.

During our senior year I returned to work embalming animals for the next new class. A few weeks after this I began having respiratory problems and had to sleep sitting up. This worried me enough to be checked by our local doctor. He determined that the formaldehyde was the culprit. I had become allergic, and that was causing the respiratory distress. He recommended I stop my work of embalming. I remained working for the department, but never again embalming animals. It didn't make me want to become an undertaker.

Anatomy was one of the toughest courses in all of the four years of study. We had to learn the bones, the muscles, the vessels and the nerve supply in each animal species. It was demanding and time consuming. In one of our first classes we were each given a box of dog bones. We had to learn all about them. One of the students looked at his pile of bones, walked out the door and never returned.

The first two years were all book work. None of the courses came easily. I had to study long hours to keep up and be prepared for all the tests. I was the oldest student in our class, having been in the war and then worked a number of years. Most of the other students were just out of high school with a couple of years of pre-vet studies in college. They were sharp! I was pretty rusty but did not lose heart.

In the third year we got to work in the clinics. This is where the study of the first two years proved necessary.

This was "hands on" work; a reward we had worked hard to achieve. Finally, we were seniors. All of our time was spent in the clinics or out on the farms, where we had hands on work with sick animals. Our three long years of commitment had gotten us this far on the path to becoming veterinarians.

During the summer between our junior and senior year we were encouraged to apply for work with a veterinarian so we could put our training into practice. Many practices were just small animal or large only. I got a job in a mixed practice, which includes work on large and small animals. Being in a mixed practice helped to learn about caring for all animals. This practice was good for me. It was a two vet practice and both men were very helpful to a green student. The one thing I had in my favor was growing up on a farm and being exposed to treating animals.

When the weekends came around these two vets told me to take care of the clinic. They were taking a couple of days off. What pressure this put on me. I was responsible for being at the clinic and also had to be prepared to go out on farm calls. I loved it! What a great way to be exposed to a good practice. This summer experience was excellent and when I got back to school in the fall I felt much more sure of myself as a veterinarian.

I completed school in eastern Washington and got a job in western Washington, in the Seattle area. This was a mixed practice, but mostly small animals. The owner was a good veterinarian and loved animals. That makes a difference.

The vet I went to work for found a house for us to rent. It was a small, two bedroom place about five miles away from the clinic. At that point we had three children and one car, so Mary Ann was left without transportation unless I drove to work and she went along with the children and had the car for the day. Life was a struggle, but we made it through these years and felt good about it. When my boss said he was going to offer me a partnership we bought our first real home.

One day my boss came in and told me that he couldn't use me anymore and to turn in my large animal supplies that I carried in my car. He didn't give me any reason. This became a difficult time for me. I searched all over the Puget Sound region for a job. No one needed another vet.

Then I found an ad in our veterinary journal for a job as a large animal clinician at Kansas State University, in Manhattan, Kansas. I called the Dean and after a long conversation he hired me.

What would we do with our home? We were able to rent it out for a year.

One of my brothers came up to our place and helped us pack up to move. It was Christmas 1958. While we were packing I received a call from our local doctor back in Idaho. He was calling to tell me that my dad had just passed away as the result of a massive heart attack. Another blow!

During World War II my dad had sold the farm. It was impossible to find any healthy men to work at that time, as most young men were in the war. It broke my heart, but my folks moved to town and bought a new home. My dad, however, was not cut out to sit around and do nothing but mow the lawn. He rented a 1,500 acre ranch up north in the Bellevue Valley. Silver Creek ran right through this place and the trout fishing was unbelievable. My brother Ed and his wife worked this farm during the summers and raised grain and cattle. In the fall we all would drive the cattle back down to the farm in Jerome. It was a great setup for a few years. Dad was soon looking for another farm to buy. He found one just a mile out of town with an old tumble-down house that he tore down, and then he built a new home.

My dad worked every day until his death at age 72. I remember telling him that when I graduated from veterinary school I would be able to make $40,000 a year. He said, with a sly look in his eye, "I just sold that many cattle." And I thought it took a college degree to be successful. He was an honest man, sincere in everything he did. His reputation in the community was undisputed. A handshake was as good as a written contract. He wasn't much of a churchgoer, although he had come from a religious family and had a brother who was a Methodist minister. Dad always gave money to the church, and now and then he attended services, but most of his Sundays were devoted to work. In his latter years he and my mom went to church a little more regularly. I believe they both loved the Lord and had given their lives to Him.

During my last years in Jerome, Dad and I rode in the Jerome posse together. We had a lot of fun, going from one rodeo to another in all of the little towns around the valley. Those are days I will never forget! My memories of my dad are all good. I hope my children might say the same someday.

We packed everything in my brother's pick up and a trailer that we pulled behind our car and headed for Idaho. I told my mom that I would stay and help her run the farm. She said, "No, you take that job. I will get along alright."

We left for Kansas right after Dad's funeral. One of my nephews and his wife drove the pickup. In a few days we were in Manhattan where the Dean had found a house for us to rent. He was a great guy and took good care of us.

I went to work as a large animal clinician. Part of my job was taking the senior students out to farms to treat the large animals. This was a fun job for me as I usually had four or five big "corn fed" students—all much bigger than I—to treat the cows, pigs or horses.

Once in awhile as we came back to town we would stop by our little house where Mary Ann had some warm cookies, milk or coffee for these hungry kids.

This was an interesting house. It was as old as the hills and was built on an old river's bottom soil. The house had settled so the owner put a jack in the basement that reached from the floor to the floor joists above. Every once in a while he would come by and jack the house up a bit. We found that if we dropped something round, like a marble, on the floor it would automatically roll to a corner of the dining room. It was a fun house in a very old and nice area of town. Next door was a house rented to four students. They liked our family and were very good to our children.

We had a screened-in porch and enjoyed sitting out there early in the morning having breakfast. There were lots of beautiful birds like cardinals and flying squirrels to entertain us. Our kids loved it!

This year proved to be good for all of us. There was one problem: we missed the mountains and the water of Puget Sound. As the school year dwindled towards summer I told the Dean we were going to move back to Washington. He wanted us to stay, but we were feeling the call to come home. The Dean thanked us for our work and wished us well.

Before leaving I found another ad in our veterinary journal—this one from Hill Packing Co., Topeka, Kansas. Hill

Packing Co. produced special diets for small animals, sold only through veterinary clinics. They were looking for someone to represent them in the Northwest. Mr. Hill wasn't around the day I drove over to Topeka but his son-in-law, Don Hogue, was in, and he was the man in charge of the company. We had a long, friendly conversation, and he hired me. He offered to pay to move everything back to Washington. He also gave me a new car to use. We were able to move right back into our home.

Everything was good again. We were back where we belonged. Our Heavenly Father was looking out for us. For three years I traveled for Hill Packing Co., covering the territory from San Francisco, through Oregon, Washington, Idaho, Montana, Nevada, Utah and Alaska. Visiting all of the clinics and hospitals in this area gave me some good ideas about building a clinic someday. It was a great job and I was pretty much my own boss.

About three years later a nice piece of property on a busy road near our home was put up for sale. Thinking it would be a good location for a clinic I bought the land. Then I went to the bank and borrowed enough to build a clinic. One of my neighbors was an architect. I hired him and his partner and they designed my clinic. We got it built.

What an exciting time this was for the Otto family! Again God had provided. No more long road trips and weeks away from home. Now I had a place of my own, a short walk from our home.

To save money while starting the practice, I decided it would be best if Mary Ann volunteered to work in the clinic. Mary Ann's mom was living with us, and she volunteered to watch the children. I twisted Mary Ann's arm, and she reluctantly agreed. It seemed to be a fine idea: now we could spend our days together as well as our nights.

One day a cat was brought in with a huge swelling on its face. After examining the swelling it was easy to determine that it was an abscess, quite common in male cats fighting over female cats. Nothing too serious. I took the cat from the owner to our treatment room with the plan to lance the abscess, drain out all of the pus and later in the day send it home with medication. "Mary Ann," I yelled, "come and help me with this cat." When she arrived in the room, I explained, "All you have to do is hold it while I lance and drain this abscess." She held the cat firmly by the scruff of the neck, and I proceeded to lance the swelling. Sounded reasonable and safe. It didn't go quite as I had expected. As I punctured the swelling with my scalpel the cat let out a loud screech and jumped out of Mary Ann's arms. He bounced off the wall, landed in the bath tub we used for bathing animals, and ran amok all around the treatment room. Finally, we were able to corner him near the cages and place him gingerly into the cage to be treated later, when his ire had settled. That day at the clinic ended Mary Ann's career as a veterinary assistant. She decided there had to be something she could do that wouldn't be so life-threatening.

A few days later she was able to get a good job (where she got paid) with the research department of Weyerhauser Company. She was the person who took care of all the research doctors working on wood products. It turned out to be an excellent job, which she enjoyed for several years.

Soon we decided to move to a home with a swimming pool. Our family would enjoy the pool and it was still quite close to the clinic. This was a good move: we had more fun and all of our neighbors became our friends. We had parties together and most of the kids were welcome in our swimming pool. Everyone knew where their children were just by the noise emanating from our backyard.

For a number of years I operated the clinic by myself. As business increased I needed some help. A fellow veterinarian in the neighborhood felt the same way, but neither of us could afford a full-time vet, so we hired a fellow and shared him equally for a long while. Eventually, I felt secure enough to hire him full-time, and later we formed a partnership with a third fellow who had a clinic nearby. His place was an old house, so he was willing to sell the property and join us. For nearly twenty years we had a good partnership.

I was the tender-hearted soul who couldn't bear to see an animal put to sleep just because the owner was moving or thought the pet had become too much bother. Usually, I would tell the owner we could keep the animal a few days as a boarder and try to find it a new home. Most people found that a workable solution. Sometimes I would take home dogs that were in this situation.

One day, at noon, I brought an Afghan home. He was a large dog with a wild disposition. He wasn't mean, just undisciplined, something that could be taken care of with a little tender care, I thought. When we got out of the car, the front door of our house was open. This dog ran into the living room, lifted his leg on our sofa and left a big puddle of urine. Not being satisfied with that, he ran out the back door, and jumped into our swimming pool. It was a warm summer day, so I couldn't chastise him for that It would not have been so bad, but he chased a neighbor and took a bite out of him, and the neighbor didn't think it was a good thing.

I loaded him back into the car and drove him back to the clinic. We never found a home for that vagabond of a dog.

This didn't cure me from bringing dogs home. The next time it was a Basenji. These little dogs were an import from Africa and cute as could be. They were short-haired, with a curly tail, ears that stood at attention and rather long slender legs, ready to run after a lion. I loved these little dogs and always wanted one but they were too expensive for me. Then one day a fellow brought one in. His name was Tongo. The owner was moving away to start a job where he would be traveling for days at a time. He couldn't keep Tongo, hated to give him up and refused to have him put to sleep. This sounded like the opportunity I had been waiting for. Casually, I suggested that I might be able to take Tongo. The owner agreed and rapidly left, never to be seen again.

I put Tongo in a cage and when the day was near closing time, I let him out for a run around inside for a little while. Everything seemed to be going smoothly so at closing time, I loaded Tongo into the car and took him home, expecting every one to be as happy as I was in getting a free dog.

He was cute and very active. Our kids liked him. He wasn't mean and got along with all of us. However, there was one problem that the owner hadn't told me about. If Tongo got out of the house, he would take off like a streak of lightning and run like the wind. And that is just what happened. Someone came in the front door and Tongo, seeing his chance, took off before the door could be closed. I had all the kids chasing after him, but he was too swift and disappeared. About the time the sun was setting, we had a call from a neighbor asking about this little curly tailed dog that was in his back yard. We rounded him up, took him home, gave him a lecture and warned everyone to watch him when the door was open. We kept Tongo for a quite a while and never cured him of running away. Even T-bone steaks were not enough to keep him home.

The next Basenji I obtained was a little female named Cheena. She had a personality much different from Tongo's. She was more content to stay home and be friends with everyone. I took her home. We all loved her, and then one day she wasn't feeling too spry. She became lethargic, refused to eat and needed to be checked over. I took her to the clinic, took blood samples, did an X-ray of her abdominal area and found an unwanted tumor. It had grown quite large, but never caused her any problems until the last few days. I talked her condition over with my two partners and we determined there wasn't anything we could do for her. A few days later, she died quietly in our back yard. There was much sadness in our home.

One of our clients was a Basenji owner. He knew his dog was one of the finest in the world and didn't want anything to happen to him. Our clinic was the only place he would bring the dog for boarding, and he would always call when he was back in town to tell us he was coming to pick up his dog. He trusted us. Well!!

One time when his dog was with us for a few days of boarding, our kennel boy accidentally left the kennel room door open. He was bringing the dogs in from the run areas, when this little guy saw the door open, jerked loose and took off. Three of us took off after him. I couldn't lose this little dog! The owner would sue me, and mean it. He was more than fond of this dog. We chased after him, up the hill, through yards and all around the neighborhood. I think he was having fun, but we were getting exhausted. Then he ran into a fenced back yard through an open gate. We followed, puffing and sweating. We captured the little escape artist, got him back to the clinic and found the owner had just called, telling our receptionist he was on his way to pick up his dog. That was a close call! We kept boarding this little dog for a few more years.

There are many other tales of veterinary practice I could talk about, as could any veterinarian who had been in practice for a few years, but I won't. It was a wonderful profession, and I am glad to be called "Doc."

During my early years of practice I belonged to an organization called The Exchange Club. The club's purpose was to help local citizens and improve the areas where we lived. One project we took on was finding a place for senior citizens to meet and enjoy life together. We found that place on the waterfront in the little town of Edmonds. It was a large building that had been used for boat building. Two brothers owned it and were willing to lease it out. It was an ideal location on the shores of Puget Sound, but it needed much work to make it into a usable space for the seniors.

The cement floor was covered with plastic material that had adhered over the years. It all had to be scraped off. To make it ready for occupancy we needed to build restrooms, install a kitchen and do extensive remodeling. We worked on weekends and every evening after dinner. Only a small group of us took on the challenge. Finally we had it ready and a dedication date was announced. The Mayor gave a speech and thanked The Exchange Club. The doors were opened and people began to arrive regularly, enjoying the comforts provided. Officers were elected, and a manager was hired.

In order to raise money we formed a theatre troupe and presented programs in the local school. In one of the plays we put on, I was a bum. I wore a derby hat and smoked a cigar. This might have been my finest moment in the acting business. And one time a group of men had to dress up as ballerinas and dance around the stage. This probably ended my acting career.

People came from all around the county because we were the only act in town at the time. Everyone who came had a wonderful time. In time we received funds from the Federal government to continue operations. Later the city was able to declare the property a permanent site for the Senior Center. This was way back in the 1960s. Finally, funds became available to tear this old building down and build a new one. I was one of the early Presidents of the Center. It was a great place and continues to this day to be one of the finest Senior Centers in all of the Puget Sound area, with a choice location, right on the waterfront.

Lunches were served and the attendance continued to grow. Then other programs were offered from games, card playing, trips, classes of all kinds including computer training. I am very proud to say I took part in the founding of the Edmonds Senior Center.

· 9 ·
HAWAII

"How lovely on the mountains are the feet of him
who brings good news, who announces peace and
brings good news of happiness, who announces sal-
vation, and says to Zion "Your God reigns!"
(Isaiah 52:7)

In our contract at the clinic we had a clause providing leave for a one year sabbatical. After seven years. I was the first to take advantage of this clause.

In looking through our veterinary journal I found an ad for a veterinarian to be the Deputy State Veterinarian for the Island of Kauai. This sounded very interesting, so I made a phone call to Hawaii and the head of the State Veterinary Department. We talked, and then I talked to my wife. I had wised up since the days of my county job.

We decided to fly over and check out Kauai. We fell in love with the island but found that we would need two thousand dollars more per year to meet our expenses. We prayed. On our way back to Honolulu we thought it best to just tell the Chief Veterinarian we could use a little more money. We did not tell him that we needed two thousand dollars a year more. He said, "I have no authority to offer you more money. I will talk to the finance people and call you."

We flew home on a Saturday, not knowing what would happen. On Monday morning we had a call from the Chief telling us he could get us two thousand dollars more a year. God is good! We felt it was what He wanted us to do.

A few days later I flew to Hawaii leaving Mary Ann home (bless her) to pack up and sell the house. She couldn't leave right away because our youngest daughter was still in high school. She did it! She sold our house, sent our furniture into storage and flew to Hawaii.

In Hawaii I was able to rent a little two bedroom home at the base of the mountain called "The Sleeping Giant." People who have been on Kauai know this mountain. It was just the right place for us, except we didn't expect all of the company we would have that year. We welcomed them all.

My first concern was finding a church. I stopped by a Christian bookstore to ask their advice. The lady told me about the Lihue Assembly of God, and I went there on my first Sunday. It was a small church with a mixed congregation: Chinese, Portuguese, Hawaiians, and people from the mainland all worshiping the Lord together. I liked this little church and I was welcomed in love. The Pastor and his wife invited me to dinner after church. He said, "Just follow me." I did, and found that their house was just a block away from the house I had rented. God is Good!

We became close friends, and when Mary Ann and Robyn arrived they became good friends too. These folks had a daughter about the same age as Robyn. We attended that church all the time we were on Kauai. I served on the Elder board, and we both sang in the choir. This is the only place in the world where I could really sing. Never before or after have I been able to carry a tune. Miracle? Maybe! Thirty-three years later we are still good friends with these fine people.

My job as Deputy Veterinarian was to check all animals that came to this island to make sure they were healthy. There were lots of hogs on this island. An order came down that we needed to blood test all of them to make sure they were healthy. This was a big job.

Once, a mule was brought to the island for the cane harvest. I had to blood test him, so some men rounded him up and put him in a barn. I attempted to get some blood from his jugular vein, but he didn't want anything to do with a needle. He'd rear up in the air, paw the air with his front feet and kick with his heels. I tried and tried. Suddenly he broke the rope and burst out of there like a bullet. He got lost in the cane field. Eventually, we caught him and got the blood.

My work was usually over about 4:00 p.m. and from then till morning I was free. This made me think about doing some other job. There was a vet clinic on the island. I went to talk to the vet in charge and told him I could work a few hours a day and on Saturday. He thought this was an answer to prayer, although he was not a praying sort of guy. I got the job. We worked well together and I treated some conditions that we had never seen on the mainland.

One of the biggest problems that dogs were having was heart worms. I had never confronted this problem. This disease was caused by mosquitoes. Heart worms would form in the blood vessels, get into the heart and plug everything up. We saw them in blood vessels from the heart, to the arteries in the back legs. Very deadly! We treated many dogs with this disease. Some were beyond treating.

More often than we would have liked, we would see a dog that had encountered a wild pig. Many local folks liked to hunt the pigs with dogs, and when the pig was cornered he would fight back. The wounds could be life threatening. Didn't see any wild pig wounds in Washington.

Sometimes we would go on large animal calls. People had saddle horses, and the owners of the cane fields had mules. There was one large ranch on Kauai that had a large herd of beef cattle. I would go out there now and then to join the cowboys (*panioles*) and herd the cattle from one pasture to another. They would give me a horse to ride. It was another way for me to enjoy Hawaii. Out in the fields there would be mango trees, and all I had to do was help myself.

We had time to enjoy the warm waters of the Pacific too. Snorkeling was always enlightening: we saw many different fish with varied colors, sizes and shapes.

Our son Randy came over to be with us when his school was out. He brought a classmate with him. The two of them got jobs painting houses. They earned their way, but when the tide was up they would abandon the painting and head for the beach. They enjoyed a terrific summer with us.

Some of my friends from high school days heard we were on Kauai, so they came for a visit. At Christmas time we had family come. Our little house had kids sleeping all over the place in sleeping bags. What a wonderful Christmas we had that year. On Christmas eve we went down to the beach and had a cookout. Wouldn't want to do that in our hometown without a heavy coat, gloves and boots.

Before we moved to Hawaii, Mary Ann had been working for Women's Aglow, a Christian organization, helping organize a trip to Israel. While we were in Hawaii, they offered to fly her to the Holy Land to help guide the tour. She wanted me to come along. I would have to pay my own way and be gone for two weeks. I talked to my boss. I had not been working long enough to accumulate leave, but he was merciful and said I could go. When the time came we flew to Tel Aviv via Seattle and New York City. When we landed, Mary Ann said it was like coming home.

We toured sites during the day. In the evenings we attended huge meetings where teaching and healing took place. On the tour bus, Mary Ann was in charge of all of us. She was accountable for our safety and keeping us together.

If there were soldiers walking down the road and they needed a ride our driver would always stop and pick them up. It may have been the law. Our driver's name was Gad (pronounced God), and our travel guide was named David. So we felt safe traveling with God and David. They were both fine people. David told us from the very beginning not to try to proselytize them. They weren't interested in becoming Christians. David was an amazing guide. He knew all of the places that Jesus had traveled and what happened at each site. He knew more about Christianity than most Christians. The trip was blessed, and another would be well worth it.

When my year of sabbatical was over we had to make a decision: would we stay on Hawaii or come back home? If we stayed I would have to sell my share in the practice. It was a difficult decision. One Monday morning Mary Ann and I were praying, kneeling at the altar in our church and asking God that we might do the right thing. The Pastor came and knelt down between us putting his arms around each of us. With tears in his eyes and a wavering in his voice he said, "As much as I hate to tell you this I feel the Lord is saying for you to return home." That settled it. The decision was made for us to come back home to Washington.

Our year in Hawaii was one of the best we'd ever had. As we prepared to leave, we were completely unaware of what the Lord had in mind for our future.

· 10 ·
CHANGING DIRECTIONS

"Whether then you eat of drink or whatever you do,
do all to the glory of God."
(I Corinthians 10:31)

A few more years passed and the practice continued to grow. Everything was going along smoothly. I arrived at retirement age, but I was still feeling good and active. "Why quit now?" I thought.

Still there was something within me saying, "You have other things to do with your life." This feeling grew, and one day I made the decision. I went to work and told my partners I wanted to sell my shares of the practice. It was a shock, but my mind was made up.

We worked it out. Our contract stated exactly how things would be divided and how much the value would be for each of us. Unfortunately, even though one of them had put the specifics into our contract, my partners thought they could pay less than we had agreed. They hired an attorney. Finally, I gave in, and gave up several thousand dollars. It almost made me bitter, which was neither the direction of my heart nor what God wanted from me. I forgave them and walked away, but our friendship was gone.

I planned to go to work as a volunteer for World Concern, a global mission helping people in impoverished countries find a better way of life. They had workers in many countries aiding the local people with medical supplies, clothing and food.

My good friend from Georgia, Dr. Leroy Dorminy, founded Christian Veterinary Medicine (CVM) as an arm of World Concern. Many Third World countries would not accept missionaries but were eager to welcome vets. I went to work for CVM, and one of the first things we did was make a trip to Africa to scout locations. Dr. Dorminy and I went to Kenya, then he and another man went to South Africa. These trips paid dividends and the doors for veterinary mission began to open.

I must have a wanderlust gene in my body. Even when I was very small I wanted to go to Africa to see all of the animals. That dream came true, and it was a fascinating journey. We drove close to lions, rhinoceros, alligators, giraffes, wild dogs, hyenas, great herds of water buffalo, antelopes and many monkeys. To see these animals living in the wild was unforgettable.

My job with CVM was to contact interested veterinarians in practice, finding out whether they would like to go on a short mission and work with established veterinarians in different parts of the world. Early on we had vets stationed in Kenya, Haiti, Bolivia and Ethiopia. Today we have them in many countries. The fastest-growing and most active mission work is in Mongolia. I worked with CVM for four years and sent out over one hundred large and small animal vets. Now, thirty years later, they send out that many in one year! They also send veterinary students and veterinary technicians.

Every person we sent on mission trips came back a changed person. Their eyes were opened to the needs in underdeveloped countries and how much good a veterinarian can do. The experience is the same for people volunteering today, and many decide to go on long-term mission work.

One of our veterinarians just came back to the United States after twenty five years in Ethiopia. All of his five kids were born in Africa.

While I was with CVM, I went on mission work to Kenya, Haiti and Bolivia. Mary Ann and I spent two weeks in Bolivia where I taught courses in ophthalmology at two different veterinary schools. Mary Ann and I stayed with a couple who had been there a few years, and the man acted as my interpreter. It was a challenging time, as there was a strike going on and all traffic was halted in the city where we lived. Bolivia is the poorest country in South America. It suffers from poor government, including politicians who rob the people. While we were there the value of the money went down so fast that each day it took bigger and bigger bags to carry fewer dollars home.

However, of all the places I have ever been, Haiti was the poorest. Haiti is filled with people living in extreme poverty, most of them without hope. I went as a veterinarian when Haiti had been plagued with a swine disease that had prompted the government to kill all of the pigs. The United States government sent a whole new stock of pigs. The plan was to give each family that wanted pigs a pregnant sow, and when she had her babies the owner was to give most of them to other families so they could start raising pigs. But the imported pigs were not adjusting to the climate and the small amount of food available, so the U.S. had to send in pig food too. It was an ambitious program and it nearly failed, like so many others do.

Haiti has more missionaries per capita than any other place in the world. I have friends who have been working there more than twenty five years, and they are still facing and working to solve the same problems. The land has been denuded of trees causing great loss of soil when it rains. The soil washes into the ocean so from the air you can see a red ring of water all around the land. The trees were destroyed by goats, and by people cutting them down for firewood. There doesn't seem to be any way out.

The U.S. has tried to assist these countries, but I wonder how much good our monetary aid programs can produce. If a country is run by greedy people who don't really care about their citizens, financial aid just feeds corruption. I prefer programs that help individuals change their lives.

A secret to the success of veterinarians in mission work is peoples' openness when a sick animal was treated and became well. People so appreciate the saving of their animal that they often allow the vet to tell them about Jesus. Many people are coming to know Jesus through this work, and it is fabulous to see people turn their dreary lives into lives filled with happiness and joy.

After four years of volunteer work I began feeling some chest pains. Not a good sign. I stopped my volunteer work. The best thing to do, I thought, was to have my doctors check me out. They did all the tests they do on heart patients, including sending some dye into the heart vessels. Sure enough several vessels were plugged with plaque. One was ninety percent closed. They sent me to the medical school at the University of Washington where they put in some stents. A few days later I was back home. Since then I have had my heart checked regularly. One time they tried to put another stent in, but it didn't work. In 2007 they put a pacemaker in my chest. This made a world of difference. Since then I have been feeling pretty perky. God is good!

Once I was feeling better I began searching for another job. I thought it would be a good idea to get a job with the U.S. Government as a meat inspector. They hired me. Must have been desperate. I went through a long period of training, starting in Colorado at a large slaughterhouse. Then they moved me to Washington and I worked in several plants.

By now people might think I was a bit crazy, with all of the jobs I have had and all of the moving we went through. As I said, I must have been born with a gene for wanderlust. Fortunately for me, my wife was willing to put up with all of these moves. What an amazing gal! Mary Ann has been extremely patient with my restlessness. She probably should have beaten me years ago.

Perhaps I was a bit crazy, but every place gave us fond memories and new friends, many of which we still enjoy. Our lives together have been good. We have a wonderful family, precious friends and a loving God.

That is why I decided to try writing a book. I have never done such a thing, but I will be happy if it turns out to be a good memory builder for my children, grandchildren and great-grandchildren.

· 11 ·
RETIREMENT

*"Return to your rest, O my soul, for the Lord
has dealt bountifully with you."*
(Psalm 116:7)

Finally, I decided to really retire. After my heart's health became an issue we decided to move from our three-level home to a condominium, so I wouldn't have to mow the lawn, paint the house or be responsible for other strenuous chores. This wasn't an easy decision, because we loved our old house ... and it was old!

We had a beautiful view looking out over Puget Sound. We could watch the Olympic Mountains and see the sun set behind them in all of its glory. We had become accustomed to the waterfront sounds: the ferry horn, announcing arrival and departure as the ferry shuttled passengers to and from the Olympic Peninsula, and the constant, deep-throated bark of sea lions vying for dominance on a platform next to the ferry landing. It was a tough decision to sell this home.

We decided to sell it ourselves. We ran ads in the papers, put up signs along the way, announced an open house and waited. A few people came by, checked it out and left. No one seemed interested. The open house was on a Sunday showing, and we knew the right people would come along. As the day wore on a few more people came by, just looking! As 5:00 p.m. was fast approaching, we began preparing to pick up our signs and call it a day. Just then a man and woman arrived to check out our house. They had just sold their home, so they were very interested. They wandered through the house checking out the bedrooms, the basement area, which also had a view of the mountains and the Sound, and the living area and kitchen. Then they talked it over between themselves and said, "We want to go get our daughter and come back again. Would you mind if we come back in a little while?" We said, with enthusiasm, that we would be happy for them to return. It wasn't long before they returned, showed the home to their daughter, had a discussion and decided on the spur of the moment to buy it. They wrote us a check for the full amount and we then had thirty days to move.

We looked around our little hometown to find a condominium that didn't have stairs and could not find one. Now it was time to expand our search area to see what was available. During this time we drove out to Mill Creek to see if there was anything available that we could afford.

Mill Creek was a very interesting area. Japanese investors had bought 1,800 acres of mostly forest land to build a complete community centered around expensive homes. Early on they built a golf course, restaurant, swimming pool and tennis court. They built beautiful homes of first-class construction, in a variety of styles. People with money came from all around the area to buy homes. If money were no object, a person would have been hard pressed to make a choice of which home to buy. The next thing the investors did was build a small shopping center along the only road to Mill Creek: banks, grocery stores, restaurants and some businesses were added. The community made for a delightful place to live, miles away from the bustle of cities. It was no place for ordinary, hard-working homeowners: it was a place folks would drive their visitors, to see how the affluent lived.

Fortunately for us, they were building a new area for condominiums at the time we were looking to move. The setting and landscaping were excellent. We visited an open house and were pleased to find it was something we could afford if we stretched a little. It was small enough for us to be comfortable in, just the two of us This was on a Sunday afternoon. We returned the next day and convinced the agent to see if the builder wouldn't come down a bit on the price. He talked to the owner and came back with a figure we could afford. The deal was made. The owner granted us the privilege of storing furniture in the garage until the house was completed. It all worked out. We had time to pack our things and get ready to move.

So it was off to Mill Creek for us. The way things worked out so smoothly showed us once more that our God had a plan for us and it wasn't over yet.

We had moved a number of times and each move helped us to meet new friends. This was another time to get acquainted with other retirees. We were all in the same boat.

There was one more house in our future. This time in Gold Creek. Why in the world would we want to move again? This time it really wasn't my idea. It was our daughter Robyn's plan. She owned a condominium down the road a ways and thought we could save money if we bought a home together and shared the expenses. The home we shared was our dream home—room for company, and plenty of room for us and our daughter. But after Mary Ann had a near-fatal accident, that home was too much to maintain. It was time to check out the possibility of moving to a retirement center.

Our daughter, Robyn, and I spent days and nights checking out the retirement centers in our area. We made a list of features we wanted, for example a washer and dryer within our apartment. Some places had them down the hallway, and that was not acceptable for us. Using this list we checked out seven different places and compared them. None were ideal. We checked out one more place, and it appeared to have most things we needed. This place had a wonderful, experienced marketing lady. She was willing to do almost anything to accommodate us. For example, we had not sold our house yet and we could not move until that was done. She told us if we would put a down payment on the books she would hold a place for us. One day she came out to our house, and we measured our furniture to see if it would fit in the new apartment. They had a two bedroom place that proved to be too small for our furniture, so we waited. Then one day she called and said she had another vacancy for us to check out. We did! Most of the units were the same drab color, but the previous tenant had painted this unit in a color we liked: green. Besides that it had nice drapery. In fact the curtains in the bedroom were of the same color and design as a chair we had. We were sold. God had provided just what we wanted.

We still had not sold our house, and it seemed to be a monstrous problem. How long would she keep this apartment reserved? We talked quite often with her and she said not to worry. It took us three months to sell our house. Then we moved in.

After I retired I got a pastor's license from the Four Square Church. This qualified me to preach and to officiate at weddings and funerals. I became the pastor for seniors at our church, and we were with that church for several years. They had a pastor at the retirement center before we moved in, then one day he disappeared. He didn't show up for the Sunday service. No one knew what happened. He was a young man who must have had other commitments. He never came back. When we moved into our retirement home they found out I was a pastor, so I was asked to serve the little church. I accepted. That was four years ago. We haven't been thrown out yet.

We had a nice room with cushioned seats and a good organ. All we needed was an organist. Soon a couple moved in, and the wife was an organist. She accepted our offer, and she has been serving here as organist for four years also. For several years we had a choir. At present we do not. Maybe again someday. This has been a great opportunity for me to study the Bible and to serve others.

Retirement can be full and satisfying if you want it to be. It does not have to be boring and dull and lifeless. It is so very important to keep active, and most folks here do. There are things to do every day, as in most retirement centers. No one needs to feel lonely. Our center is especially friendly to everyone.

We have a large bus that takes people everywhere. Once a week they have a "mystery ride" that goes wherever the driver wants to wander. Folks really enjoy these outings. We go to events around the area, mostly in the evenings. Live theater is always good and programs at our local events center are most interesting. There is no reason to be lonely or inactive, unless your body says no. And that happens to all of us at times. As a community we are all friends and concerned about each other. We wouldn't go back to owning our own home with all of the upkeep. This was a good move!

We will live here for we-don't-know-how-many years in the future, but here we are, and still very happy together.

· 12 ·
OUR ADULT FAMILY

*"Behold, children are a gift of the Lord; The fruit
of the womb is a reward. Like arrows in the hand
of a warrior, so are the children of one's youth. How
blessed is the man whose quiver is full of them."*
(Psalm 127: 3, 5a)

Family has always been very important to us. We have
tried to raise our children to be honest and have a
good work ethic. So, when we had our clinic they all had a
chance to work in it. Cleaning cages was their main job and
one that taught them humility. It is a humble job to clean up
after cats and dogs. We also tried to be faithful in our church
attendance. At one period of time Mary Ann and I were
Sunday School teachers. Later we ran the youth program.

We tried to do as many things as possible together as a
family. It wasn't always easy. There were times when we were
ready to go on an outing and I would get a phone call. Something like this: "Dr. Otto, my little Boo is having trouble
whelping. Won't you come to the clinic?" So the trip was
postponed and off to the clinic I went to help this little dog
have her puppies. Our kids usually forgave me for this type
of interruption.

We tried to attend events at school in which they were
involved. I would sneak away from work on days when my
son was playing football. I believe it made him feel good to
look across the sideline and see his dad rooting for his team.
The most exhilarating times for me were when we would all
go skiing. That was my wintertime passion.

I loved to ski in the snowy mountains of Idaho and Washington. When my kids were in junior high we started them in ski school. The schools took the kids to the ski slopes every Saturday morning. They didn't mind getting up at 5:30 a.m. to catch the bus, nor getting home at 6:00 or 7:00 p.m., tired and worn out. They got to the point where they could ski well enough to go with old Dad on ski outings. We skied most of the slopes in Washington and, of course, Sun Valley, Idaho. Sun Valley had become one of my favorites over the years due to both great skiing and good memories from my younger days. What a great time we had, and our fellowship was family building. Our kids have turned out to be great adults with good values. Maybe skiing with old Dad had something to do with it. I had to give up skiing at age 78, but I will never give up the beautiful memories.

We have been blessed to do things with our children as adults too. Regina was a travel agent in Kansas City and one summer she was able to take her mom on a trip to Europe. They toured Switzerland, Austria and northern Italy. It was a fascinating trip for both of them. That was a number of years ago and they still talk about it. What memories.

Randy and I have been on several trips together. Our first trip was to Kenya. We wanted to visit our good friends, Kit & Jan Flowers, who were serving as missionaries for Christian Veterinary Mission. They were stationed way out in the countryside working with the Masai people. It was a long trip from Nairobi to their home, over roads that were filled with potholes. It was impossible to drive down these roads without hitting a hole and bouncing along to the next one. We were excited to be in this beautiful country and to enjoy the countryside and the native people.

While driving our rented car down the road, far out in the middle of nowhere, the engine just gave up. Neither of us had the slightest idea what was wrong. We were standing around hopeless and helpless waiting for a miracle to happen. After a few lonely minutes an Englishman came along with two Kenyans with him. They stopped to check on us, which was a very friendly thing to do. This man asked us what seemed to be the trouble and we told him the car had just stopped. Instantly they knew what was wrong. One of the Kenyans crawled under the car, took the gas line apart, emptied the glass jar that the gas flowed through and then sucked on the gas line. He would get a big mouthful of gas, spit it out and do it again. Soon he had the line cleared, and the car was ready to go. They told us this was not an unusual occurrence because of all the dust and dirt, and the poor quality of gas. The gas lines would get plugged up to the point where there wasn't any gas flowing to the engine.

We thanked them and offered them some money for their effort. No way would they accept that. They did accept our thanks and then drove away in a cloud of dust. I'll bet we might have still been there if these good people hadn't come along. Maybe not. Everyone in Kenya seemed to be extremely helpful.

We had driven down the road a number of miles when the car stalled again. This time we knew what to do and Randy did the sucking out of the gas line. I had to stand guard as we were right in the middle of a large group of monkeys, not the friendly kind. Fortunately, they never came too close to us and we got the car going again.

After a number of miles we finally arrived at the compound where our friends lived. They had a nice little home that they and their two daughters shared. Everyday there would be Kenyans coming to their home to ask for food or help of some kind. Randy and I would jump into the Land Rover with Kit and head out into the country to visit some villages. Everywhere we went the people knew Kit. He had a reputation of loving these people and always was willing to help them out. His main duty was to treat the sick animals, and there were lots of them. Parasitism was one of the most common problems. He would give the animal a shot that killed the parasites, and in a few days that animal would begin putting on weight. Because animals were so important to their livelihood they began trusting Kit. When he would save an animal, it would draw him closer to the owner, and he could tell the family about Jesus. Bringing folks into the kingdom of God was easier for veterinarians than for most missionaries, because they bonded with people over issues of life and death.

While we were with Kit, he took us to a village and we drank coffee with them in their little huts. It was a challenge, as there was no sanitation available. Bravely, we would partake and even enjoy the drinks. The Kenyan people were very giving and loving, unless you were from another tribe. Then there could be trouble.

Later on back at the compound we helped Kit and the Kenyan men build a church. Our job was to help as much as possible. It was an open church with poles supporting the roof and no walls, at least during our stay. The floor was dirt and the benches were rather quaint. It served the purpose for a place to worship. The Masai people would come from miles around to worship the Lord, with Kit preaching in their language.

Our time with Kit and Jan was most enjoyable, but it had to come to an end. We had to return to Nairobi and fly home. It didn't turn out to be that easy. We had reservations on a British airline to fly to London. The flight was canceled. We stayed at the airport until we found another flight out; however, this made us late for our connecting flight from London. We had to stay another night there. Finally, we found a flight to New York, then across the country to our home state of Washington. That trip to Kenya was well worth it. We have many good memories.

Another year brought another adventure. This time it was Randy and me, going to the land of the gentle people of New Zealand. This trip started off very well, with our being granted seats in first class! It was such a long trip, and this seating proved comfortable. We were very thankful.

Upon our arrival in Auckland we rented a car and took off. We did had no definite plans. The one thing we knew was that we wanted to drive to Christ Church, on the South Island, to stay overnight. That was our plan! Otherwise we planned to go wherever the wind blew us or the spirit led us.

It was a long but interesting drive through beautiful countryside dotted with little towns. We arrived in Christ Church and searched for a bed-and-breakfast (B&B) or a small hotel. After checking into a nice little hotel, we went out for dinner at a small restaurant and drove around the city before turning in for the night. The next morning we awoke early, had breakfast and took off to go to the southernmost part of the island. We saw many beautiful farms that had herds of deer: there were deer everywhere!

The land was beautiful, and the people were extremely helpful in telling us about places to visit. Our traveling was casual, with no specific destination, so we stayed in B&Bs along the way. The lady who operated one of them had a computer, and I asked her if she would send an e-mail to my wife. She said she certainly would! That was the quickest way to communicate with home, and I really appreciated her effort and cooperation.

Finally, we arrived at the southernmost point on the South Island. We heard that a small cruise vessel was taking a group of people out, so we joined a few other folks for this overnight trip. The waters were calm and the food delicious! After a few hours the captain stopped the boat and said we could take kayaks out for an hour or so. Without hesitation, Randy and I each got a kayak and paddled our way into the deep waters. It was near evening, the waters were calm, the moon was beginning to rise and all was well. It was a high-light for us. After a night aboard the cruise vessel, floating in quiet waters, we headed back to port. Breakfast was another wonderful meal. We learned to like New Zealanders' food!

From here we drove into the mountains along the west coast of the South Island. We would stop now and then for a hike into the woods. We didn't see any wild animals. Our trip north took a couple of days until we reached the northern part of this Island and crossed the waters to Wellington on the southern tip of the North Island. Traveling further north we came to a Maori village. They were living just as they had for years. There were hot water vents where the Maoris cooked their food. These were wonderful people with hearts as big as all outdoors. They put on a theater program that showed us how the Maoris lived. Most interesting.

From here we traveled up the east coast of the North Island. We found a very nice B&B in a small village. Ours was near the water and a port where many personal boats were moored. We learned much about the history of this part of the islands. We were so glad that we had the chance to visit New Zealand. It was a hurried trip, but very fascinating. Another memory builder.

Our trip home was not quite as comfortable as our trip to New Zealand. We sat in the back of the plane among a group of fellows who were noisy and rowdy. There was no way to sleep. This turned out to be a long and miserable flight home to Seattle, but as I look back upon it I just want to remember the good things. Just the two of us, Dad and Son traveling together and sharing our lives. It was good. It would be nice to go back and spend more time in New Zealand; enough time to get to know the people better and maybe have a chance to stay on a sheep ranch or a deer farm. Such beautiful country.

One day while sitting around twiddling my thumbs I received a letter telling of a trip to Germany for ex-POW's. As I read through the material it seemed like a great idea to take this trip. I called Randy in Alaska and asked him if he would like to take another trip with his dad. He jumped at the chance. We were going back to the prison camp at Stalag Luft IV.

We made our plans to fly to New York and meet the other people going on this trip. It turned out to be a large group, but only three of us were from Stalag Luft IV. The rest of the crowd, about fifty people, were going to visit Stalag Luft 1, which had been an internment camp for officers. No enlisted men had been sent there. Many of the officers took their families on this trip. After an overnight in New York we flew directly to Zurich, Switzerland. From there we flew to Berlin. We stayed in a nice hotel for a couple of nights and then took a tour bus, north to Poland and Stalag Luft IV. Our bus was comfortable and in the rear there was a table we could sit around to visit.

Along on this trip were John Nichol and Tony Rennell, two British writers. In conversation with them we learned that John was a navigator on a Tornado bomber in the first Gulf War. They had been shot down by a SAM missile in the desert of Iraq. On the flyleaf of John's book, *Tornado Down*, he writes:

> "They became extraordinary when their tortured faces, battered almost beyond recognition by their Iraqi interrogators, flashed across the world's television screens. In that instant they became the symbol of Saddam Hussein's brutal regime, an image of suffering that was engraved on the public's mind.
>
> Tornado Down is their story. It is a graphic and painfully honest account of the hectic build up to war."

John was the right person to write about the POW's in Germany. He knew about imprisonment. He too had suffered and struggled for survival.

As we traveled north on the bus to Stalag Luft IV, I sat with John and Tony around that table in the back of the bus to discuss my own life as a POW.

John and Tony were both taking down notes hurriedly as well as taping our conversation. Randy sat there with us taking it all in. Most of the things I was talking about, he had never heard before. There were two other POW's with us, George Guderly and Roger Allen. We are all included in the book *The Last Escape* written by John and Tony. We have all become friends after this time together.

As soon as we arrived at our destination close to Stalag Luft IV we had a good meal and signed into our hotel. The next day we drove out to the site of the camp. The Polish people had created a memorial near where Stalag Luft IV had been. Now it has all returned to a forest. All of the buildings are gone, and only a few pieces of foundation are visible. This area had belonged to the Polish government before the Germans took over. After the war this area was exchanged for another section of land someplace else so the Poles reclaimed their land. The Polish people had built a cement replica of an American airman at this place. We had the honor of planting some trees along the path to the memorial.

We did not know what to expect when we arrived at this site. What we found was that the whole population of the little village nearby had come out for this celebration. The mayor of the town welcomed us and gave a long speech in Polish. There was a forty-man honor guard from the Army along with a number of Marines and sailors. Music was played, and we were asked to lay wreaths at the foot of the memorial statue. The Polish people there loved the Americans and showed us their love. Everyone wanted to shake our hands and thank us for our service. It was a very heartwarming experience for three old warriors.

It was a wonderful time, and it brought back many not-so-pleasant memories. We saw the path through the forest where our long march had begun. This brought back the terrible memories of those months of horrific suffering and the struggle for survival. But, we three made it home.

After our day here we jumped in the bus and returned to Berlin. From that time on we became tourists and joined with all of the other POW's for a tour. We visited Nürnberg, Salzburg, Austria and Berchtesgaden, Hitler's retreat high on a mountain top.

While on a bus trip we heard over the radio about the planes crashing into those two towering buildings in New York City. Air traffic came to a screeching halt. John Nichol was back in England and was planning to come for our farewell dinner and be our guest speaker. He couldn't get back. We never saw him or Tony Rennell again. In Nürnberg we had a wonderful farewell dinner at an old castle. We were ready to return home, but our tour guide, who was also a veteran of WWII, was very worried about our flights. He thought they all might be canceled. After much investigation and checking with the airlines he found that all of our flights were on time. We could go home. Two tired travelers made it back to Seattle with lots to talk about and explain to our families. I am so very glad that my son and I were able to make this trip together. Randy had learned, for the first time, of all these things that had taken place in my life. I had never, ever talked about my days as a POW. This was not unusual for men and women coming home from a war. Many veterans tried to forget what they had been through in wartime, and forgetting meant not talking about these experiences. This applies to those who fought in Vietnam and in the Middle East, and yet, real healing only comes about when these experiences are shared.

This had been one of the most reflective trips abroad I had ever taken. I had no idea what was going to be in store for me some seven years later.

The most fascinating trip I have ever taken took place in October 2008. All three of our children went with me to Austria. It was a time to meet new folks who had seen me in the past and to be honored by the local state (Styria) government. What an honor. I am proud we had this opportunity to travel to Austria and to meet some of the nicest people in the world.

· 13 ·
KINDRED SPIRITS

*"And hope does not disappoint because the love of
God has been poured out within our hearts through
the Holy Spirit, Who was given to us."
(Romans 5:5)*

*1944, our time of imprisonment,
to 2008, a time of renewing.*

My how time flies. Most of my past life had faded
into dimness as I was more interested in the present and the future than those things that had gone before.
At age 86 I thought it was time to take things easy and coast
the rest of my days.

I am still busy preaching a sermon every Sunday and taking a day or two during the week to prepare it. This seemed
to be enough for me. There were other activities to get involved in when life slowed down and became a wee bit stuffy.
During our second year at the retirement center I became
the Treasurer for the Residents' Council. This council was
an independently functioning group involving all of the residents. We met once a month to talk over what was going on,
and discuss whether there was anything we could change to
make life a little bit better. Most monthly meetings involved
having an outside speaker come in to give us the latest information on his or her area of expertise. These speakers were
those who were involved and interested in things that senior
citizens had an interest in. The meetings were quite lively
with exchanges among the residents. After a year and one
half I was replaced as Treasurer. Since that time I have been

rather quiet, except for church involvement. We have thirty to forty regular attendees at our worship service. Many folks who are able to drive go to their own churches, except when it snows; then we have a full house.

One day in January of 2008 I received an e-mail from the son of the engineer on our B-24 bomber. He said he was browsing the internet and saw a notice from a man in Austria who was looking for POW's who had been shot down in their local area. He thought I might be interested. I was!

Suddenly there rushed through my mind the recollections of those days as a POW. Up until then, most of the events that had taken place were stored away somewhere in my brain, never to be thought of again. Some of it had come back when Randy and I returned to Stalag Luft IV. After that visit, I had thought it best to let those memories be put to rest. Why bring up ugly things? With the internet notice looking for POW's, they reared up again, maybe to haunt me.

Today, as I sit at my desk in December and look out at the snow, it reminds me of our long march through the snow and cold in Germany. Today it is 19 degrees; very cold for our part of the world. During the winter months of 1944-1945 it was every bit as cold. In fact it was bitter cold as we plodded along to our unknown destination. Wind and snow made it unbearable at times.

I remembered that everyone suffered frozen feet and hands. Some men, in extreme pain, could walk no further. Frostbite was epidemic. Maybe even worse was the dysentery. It was caused by drinking contaminated water, the only water available. It was water that had been tromped through by others going before us; water that had run off from fields men had, of necessity, used as toilets. A doctor was with our group, but without medicines he couldn't help much. I was one of the fortunate ones. When I had an attack of dysentery, I found a charcoal stick to chew on, and it cleared up my dysentery. But for most, the dysentery just got worse. Men became dehydrated from extreme loss of fluids. Day after day the dysentery took its toll, as men fell by the wayside. It was horrible.

I remembered that we were no longer the strong semi-healthy guys that had been in Stalag Luft IV. Even there, before leaving on the march, most of the men had lost fifteen to twenty pounds; from the beginning we were weakened to some degree. We continued to move along. Every day we made less mileage and every one of us became a little weaker.

I remembered that our feet were constantly wet and cold, leading to blisters. Walking was becoming more difficult day by day, made worse by frostbite and then blisters. Men hobbled and limped along as best they could. The guards were in the same situation, maybe even worse since most were elderly men who had seen much service in the front lines.

I remembered that injuries became infected and gangrene set in. Under good conditions it would have been necessary to amputate, but these weren't good conditions and there were no surgical facilities available. As a result, some of these men did lose their feet after they were returned to American forces.

I remembered that other diseases that struck us were pneumonia, diphtheria, pellagra, typhus, trench foot, and tuberculosis. All of these were later noted in medical reports. No wonder we were seeing our group shrink day after day, as men collapsed along the way. If they were lucky they were picked up by a wagon. Others died where they fell. It was hard to see your friends fall down, unable to get up. Most of us tried to help others, but we were all pretty weak. We could not carry another person far, even if two of us were trying. Our strength was disappearing rapidly.

That any of us survived is a miracle. I believe God gave us the strength to keep going.

My life was spared. I made it back home, but to this day there are residual effects. For example my hands and feet are always cold. When folks shake hands with me they always say, "Oh my, your hands are so cold." When my heart condition became apparent, the Veterans Administration increased my disability, stating that my time in prison camp and the long hard march were responsible.

Senator John Warner of Virginia delivered the following speech, which was entered into the Congressional Record of the 104th Congress in 1995:

Mr. Warner: "Mr. President, today we commemorate the 50th anniversary of the end of World War II in Europe. Victory in Europe is one of the milestone dates of this century. I rise today to honor a group of Americans who made a large contribution to the allied victory in Europe while also enduring more than their fair share of personal suffering and sacrifice: the brave men who were prisoners of war.

I believe it is appropriate to commemorate our World War II POW's by describing one incident from the war that is emblematic of the unique service rendered by those special people. This is the story of an 86 day, 488 mile forced march that commenced at a POW camp known as Stalag Luft IV, near Grosstychow, Poland, on February 6, 1945 and ended in Halle, Germany on April 26, 1945.

The ordeal of 9,500 men, most of whom were U.S. Army Air Force Bomber Command Non-Commissioned officers, who suffered through incredible hardships on the march yet survived, stands as an everlasting testimonial to the triumph of the American spirit over immeasurable adversity and of the indomitable ability of camaraderie, teamwork, and fortitude to overcome brutality, horrible conditions, and human suffering.

Bomber crews shot down over axis countries often went through terrifying experiences even before being confined in concentration camps. Flying through withering flak, while also having to fight off enemy fighters.

The bomber crews routinely saw other aircraft in formations blown to bits or turned into fiery coffins. Those who were taken POW had to endure their own planes being shot down or otherwise damaged sufficiently to cause the crews to bail out. Often crew mates – close friends – did not make it out of the burning aircraft. Those lucky enough to see their parachutes open, had to then go through a perilous descent amid flak and gunfire from the ground. Many crews were then captured by incensed civilians who had seen their property destroyed or had loved ones killed or maimed by allied bombs.

Those civilians at time would beat, spit upon, or even try to lynch the captured crews. And in the case of Stalag Luft IV, once the POW's had arrived at the railroad station near the camp, though exhausted, un-fed, and often wounded, many were forced to run the two miles to the camp at the point of bayonets. Those who dropped behind were either bayoneted or bitten on the legs by police dogs, and all that was just the prelude to their incarceration where they were under-fed, overcrowded, and often maltreated.

In February 1945, the Soviet offensive was rap-idly pushing toward Stalag Luft IV. The German high command determined that it was necessary that the POW's be evacuated and moved into Germany. But by that stage of the war, German material was at a premium, and neither sufficient rail cars nor trucks were available to move prisoners. Therefore the deci-sion was made to move the allied prisoners by foot instead of by rail or vehicles.

The 86-day march was, by all accounts, savage. Men who for months, and in some cases years, had been denied proper nutrition, personal hygiene, and medical care were forced to do something that would be difficult for well-nourished healthy, and appropri-ately trained infantry soldiers to accomplish.

The late Dr. (Major) Leslie Caplan, an American flight surgeon who was the chief medical officer for the 2,500 man section C from Stalag Luft IV, summed up the march. *It was a march of great hardship. We marched long distances in bitter weather and on starvation rations. We lived in filth and slept in open fields or barns. Clothing, medical facilities and sanitary facilities were utterly inadequate. Hun-dreds of men suffered from malnutrition, dysentery, tuberculo-sis and other diseases.*

A number of American POW's on the march did not survive. Others suffered amputations of limbs or appendages while many more endured maladies that remained or will remain with them for the rest of their lives. For nearly 500 miles and over 86 days enduring unbelievably inhumane conditions the men from Stalag Luft IV walked, limped, and in some cases crawled onward until they reached the end of their march, with their liberation by the American 104th Infantry Division on April 26, 1945.'

Unfortunately, the story of the men of Stalag Luft IV, replete with tales of the selfless and often heroic deeds of prisoners looking after other prisoners and helping each other to survive under deplorable conditions, is not well known. I therefore rise today to bring their saga of victory over incredible adversity to the attention of my colleagues. I trust that these comments will serve as a springboard for a wider awareness among the American people of what the prisoners from Stalag Luft IV—and all prisoners of war camps—endured in the pursuit of freedom.

I especially want to honor three Stalag Luft IV veterans who endured and survived the march. Cpl. Bob McVicker, a fellow Virginian from Alexandria. S/Sgt. Ralph Pippens of Alexandria, LA. And Sgt. Arthur Duchesneau of Daytona Beach. FL who brought this important piece of history to my attention, and provided me with in-depth information [including] testimony by Dr. Caplan, articles, personal diaries and photographs. Mr. McVicker, Mr. Pippens and Mr. Duchesneau, at different points along the march were each too impaired to walk under their own power. Mr.

McVicker suffered frostbite to the extent that Dr. Caplan told him along the way, that he would likely lose his hands and feet. Miraculously, he did not. Mr. Pippens was too weak from malnutrition to walk on his own during the final stages of the march, and Mr. Duchesneau almost became completely incapacitated from dysentery. By the end of the march all three men had lost so much weight that their bodies were mere shells of what they had been prior to their capture. Mr. McVicker, for example, at 5 feet 8 inches weighed but 80 pounds. Yet they each survived mostly because of the efforts of the other two.

Mr. President, I am sure my colleagues join me in saluting Mr. McVicker, Mr. Pippens, Mr. Duichesneau, the late Dr. Caplan, the other survivors of Stalag Luft IV marches, and all the brave Americans who were prisoners of war in World War II. Their service was twofold; first as fighting men putting their lives on the line each day in the cause of freedom and then as prisoners of war, stoically enduring incredible hardships and showing their captors that the American spirit cannot be broken, no matter how terrible the conditions. We owe them a great debt of gratitude and the memory of their service our undying respect."

That report is about one group of men from Stalag Luft IV. I don't know how many groups of men were moved out, but each group went in a different direction and ended up in different camps. Our group of several hundred marched for 500 miles and ended in a completely different camp.

There were nearly 10,000 men in Stalag Luft IV. Some of the weakest were taken out by train to their destination. The rest of us had to march. All of us suffered, just as these three men did. Some survived and some died along the way. No matter how you look at it, everyone suffered to the extreme.

· 14 ·
AUSTRIA

"You shall not take vengeance, nor bear any grudge against the sons of the people, but you shall love your neighbor as yourself. I am the Lord.
(Leviticus 19:18)

A few pages back I mentioned an e-mail my friend found while browsing the internet. I sat down and wrote to Josef Schutzenhofer in Poellau, Austria to find out what he was doing and why he wanted to get in contact with an American airman who had been shot down near his village.

A letter came right back and here is what he said:

"I am pleased to be in contact with a survivor of a WWII crew member whose fate is linked to the town of Poellau. Your story has a special meaning to us here in Austria, even though many do not understand or want to understand the valid deeds the allies have bestowed on us during WWII.

As an artist, a U.S. Navy veteran and long time U.S. resident I have attempted to realize my obligation on this matter and started to look at the local circumstances of WWII and how the native Austrians have dealt with their past. My finding is that there were too many willing participants in the Nazi agenda. As the war was over, they assumed a democratic exterior and remained at the core authoritarian, racist and intolerant towards anyone deviant to the status quo.

I feel that the efforts which the Americans and the Allies put forth in liberating this soiled land, were never credited in a proper manner. This is especially true for the region of Poellau.

Thus I find it especially important to keep such stories as the crew of the *Texarkana Hussy* plane had experienced, in the public ear.

In this regard I have started with a group of academics to compile documents and interviews dealing with the four USA AAF planes which crashed in close proximity to the town where I now live. We have set a goal in designating a public site upon which an art object to commemorate the event is to be placed, as well as assembling the content and framework for an exhibition on this long overdue subject.

The *Texarkana Hussy* crash is to be included in our quest and we have found a number of facts on the matter and are still searching for more.

In your letter you stated that I have located the tail section of the plane, this is misinterpretation and I must correct it. We have found some parts of a B 24 but we are not entirely sure to which of the planes these parts and pieces belong. To enable you to make a picture of our work for yourself, I will include a number of copies of our recordings, they are listed as follows:

(I, Bob, must insert here that the Texarkana Hussy was the plane that I was on and it did crash near this area.)

1. Local map/Poellau and surroundings, with marked location of crash.

2. Map of eastern section of Styria/ southeastern Austria.

3. Photo crash site of cockpit section (taken in 2007).

4. Photo of crash site of engines (taken in 2007).

5. Photo of crash site of a wing (taken in 2007).

6. Village pub of Mr. Mauerhofer (eyewitness).

7. Historic photo of tail section of *Texarkana Hussy* (1 month after crash).

8. Historic photo of tail rudders, photo taken shortly after crash.

9. Page from the town chronicle of Poellau.

10. Texarkana crew member (possibly Earl Sullivan).

11. The MACR report is conflicting. A statement describes that Earl Sullivan could not jump free of the plane and crashed with it. Other statements indicates that Sullivan did not wear a parachute since he was very tall and there was very little space in the nose cone position remains of USAAF crew member, one can make out various gun and armament parts. Other photo of a grave site could pertain to either *Texarkana Hussy* or the Halderman plane.

12. Circumstance of crash, data of plane (German text)

13. Translation of 12.

14. Interview with Mr. Peter Mauerhofer, translation from German.

15. Brochure showing the region of Poellau.

So far this is the status of our findings concerning the fate of the *Texarkana Hussy*. As a source we were able to obtain the MACR, had a brief viewing of the town chronicle of Poellau and were able to interview Mr. Mauerhofer and Mr. Zangl. Both individuals were children at the time of the incident, their access to the crash site at the time was limited, thus I believe their accounts as useful, but none the less as secondary information that has been altered and augmented over the years.

Furthermore I have a certain amount of distrust towards their statements.

There are still others who we would like to impose questions to and intend to do so this year.

In any case I am very thankful that you have contacted me with your story and the offer to provide information, such that we would have never had access to via our local contacts and findings.

There are of course numerous questions I would like to ask but I will start with a few.

- Your plane was hit over the target site, how long there after did you remain with the formation?
- After your plane dropped the bombs in Moosbierbaum, were the planes again attacked by German fighters?
- What was the weather condition?
- Do you recall the features of the landscape upon which you landed?
- Were you injured?

- Did other crew members land near you?
- At what point did you have contact with native civilians?
- How were you treated? Do you recall their character?
- How far from the plane did you land?
- How were you brought into town?
- Do you recall features of the town?
- How long were you kept on site before being transferred to Graz?

I do understand that all these questions can be overwhelming and time consuming to deal with, thus answer at your leisure. I'll be grateful for any supplementary information. Thanks for suggesting the book, *The Last Escape*. I have ordered it from Amazon."

I wrote right back to Josef and answered all of his questions to the best of my ability. All of the work he had done was impressive, and I felt obligated to help him with the project. He was sincere in his search for all of the facts concerning the planes that had crashed near Poellau. The more we communicated the more interested I became in trying to supply the missing parts for him to put together.

Through our writing back and forth we became more understanding of each other. I told him about my life as a veterinarian. He told me about a veterinarian friend of his who works for the state and said we would hit if off if we ever had a chance to meet. (The friend speaks English—a big help for me!)

I also told him about my family and he told me about his wife and son. His wife, Janice, is an American. He met her while living in America.

Following my reply to his letter, Josef sent another letter to me and here are parts of it:

"Recently I met with the König family of Poellauberg, they are the proprietors of the village inn in the Poellauberg region. *Mr. König is the grandson of the man responsible for bringing you down into the village of Poellau for detainment.* He was quite surprised to hear that after so much time in passing we were able to contact the American flier, who so briefly appeared in the regions chronology of the events . I have not told him of your plans to visit the region, but when the time seems suitable, I will impress upon him that he owes you a beer or two."

During our correspondence I mentioned to Josef that my son and I would love to come for a visit one day. Nothing definite; it was just something that we would really like to do … someday.

Josef continues:

"On not so pleasant terms as above, are the dealings with the mayoral office of Poellau in regard to our art project. My plan to install the Harry Moore painting on a public site and in close proximity to the local WWII memorial, was halted by a mayor who aspires to be politically incorrect and fosters a rather sloppy image as to his nation's involvement during the war. Over the years he has never been a supporter of our cause and wishes nothing more than that the painting would simply go away. His wish was granted and I withdrew my plans to install the work here in Poellau.

We have also regrouped our plans in that the painting will be part of an exhibition at the state legislative complex in Graz. The subject of the various crashes in Poellau is taken up by a local school class. These young people have an enthusiastic curiosity and they wish to construct an object which is to serve as an indicator point at the crash site of Harry Moore.

Franz Brugner, a local teacher, took his class to the crash site and also had an eyewitness tell of her account of the events.

It is not often that teenagers become personally involved in historical research, but the group decided spontaneously to build a small commemorative object as a memorial to the fallen airmen. The wooden structure would be in the form of a triangle covered partially with aluminum from the crashed airplane. The triangular shape was to symbolize the triangularly shaped flag which is laid upon the coffin of every fallen U.S. soldier. Hans Wiesenhofer provided the aluminum from the downed plane, The Ramp Tramp.

The instruction for the construction of this art object comes from an American artist, Douglas Hoagg. By coincidence I went to grad school with Doug in Baltimore.

Even more interesting is that his father was stationed during the war in Italy and flew missions as a B-24 gunner into Austria. I would say that he is best suited to be the lead instructor for this project. Of course we will keep you posted as to the progress on this matter.

The photo I sent you shows a group of trees right near the Inn of Mr. König with a view facing south. This site shown also marks the path taken by the crippled *Texarkana Hussy* shortly before it broke up. It must also have been the site for you and your colleagues to abandon the ship.

The additional picture shows the site where the various sections of the plane came crashing into a wooded lot and onto the field.

I have shared our correspondence with my family and friends and they are all interested in our project and would welcome a visit from yourself and your son."

In my reply to Josef I told him a little bit about my family, my veterinary practice, my wanderings around the world and work with Christian Veterinary Mission.

In another letter I told him about the story reported by Lt. Herbert Hawkins, a pilot flying alongside of our plane. He had wondered how we ever got far enough to drop our bombs. As we dropped out of the formation he saw the plane explode in mid-air.

The students who took on the art project to build an artwork honoring Harry Moore and his crew was completed and installed near a forest. It is a triangular work covered with aluminum from their crashed plane with all of the names of the crew inscribed in the aluminum. It will be there as a remembrance for many, many years. It is called *On This Foreign Field*.

As time went by we finally determined that we could communicate on the internet. What a difference that made.

Now we could be in daily touch with each other. His work progressed and he met a number of times with the Vice-Governor of Styria, Hermann Schutzenhoefer. Hermann decided it would be the right thing to do to invite me to come and they would pay my airfare.

In our earlier writings back and forth, I talked about coming to visit in Austria, thinking it might be next year. Then when things seemed to be spiraling around much faster than anticipated I thought we could come sometime in October. It turned out that in early October it was election time in Austria, not a good time to come. Finally, we arrived at a date that would accommodate everyone and when I heard that the government would pay for my airfare, it made me re-think the whole trip. Now it seemed possible that I could take all three of our children. (My wife's health would not permit her to travel these long distances). When I called each one and said I would like to take them with me to Austria and asked, "Could you come?" All three announced with great enthusiasm that they could.

Randy and Robyn had to arrange their work schedules. It all fell into place. Regina Ann, our travel agent, was able to make all of the flying arrangements.

The more I thought about all of this, the more I became convinced that God was right in the middle, working things out, transparent to us. How in the world could this have all come together, across thousands of miles in such a quick order? Who could have convinced Herr Herman Schutzenhoefer that it would be a good idea to pay for my airfare and later decide it would be right to pay for our housing?

As I look back sixty-four years to the time I was one of many prisoners of war who were trudging through the snow and cold and mud for seventy days and five hundred miles, I ask, "Who was it that kept me going?" I know it wasn't my strength alone, for that strength was about to run out. It had to be God. Every day, as we struggled to survive, He was there putting something in me that said, "Yes, you can keep on going." "Yes, you will make it." Yes, you will make it home."

I believe now, and I believed then that it was God who saved my life. Not my faith, but His grace and mercy. And I have thanked him over and over many times for His wonderful care and protection. And here, sixty four years later his grace and mercy are still guiding and taking care of me. That is the kind of a God that I believe in.

Now how was I going to pay for my children's airfare? Mary Ann and I are not rich!

The answer came loud and clear, "Cash in your IRA." I did, and it was sufficient to cover all our expenses. Thank you Lord! It was well worth it to have our three children there with me. Thank you, my loves, for making this trip one to remember forever!

Those were our plans falling into place and across the waters Josef and Janice were making plans for everything to fall into place in Austria. They asked me whether we would like to stay in a guest house in town or in a home across the street from them. We chose the home and everything turned out better than anyone could have dreamed of. The Polzhofers, Franz and Gerti,were perfect hosts. We couldn't have chosen any better.

OUR AUSTRIAN FRIENDS

Although we were only in Austria for a short period of time, it was long enough to build some solid friendships that we still enjoy.

When we arrived at our home-away-from-home, graciously provided by Franz and Gerti Polzhofer, we took a brief rest to recover from the long flight. Josef, Janice and their son, Louie, then took us to Schreiner's in Poellau for dinner and to meet some of their close friends.

Johannes and Renata Schreiner are the owners of a gasthaus that has been in their family for three generations. In 1794 there was a fire that destroyed the building, but it was rebuilt and is well kept to this day. This couple could speak English, and that made it much easier for us. (We, as Americans, were very inefficient in our host country's language. If I'm fortunate enough to visit again, I plan on studying German first.) They opened their restaurant just for us that evening. Johannes described the menu of the day, and we each ordered what seemed to appeal to our tastes. The food was delicious.

Before we had finished eating other folks started to arrive. One of the first was Johannes' father, a man my age who wanted to visit and practice his English. He had been in the German army so we had something in common; two old war veterans. We had a very good visit as others arrived.

All of them came to visit with the Americans. Some remembered the day sixty-four years earlier when our bomber crashed and they saw men coming down in parachutes. Most of them were young children at the time, but their memories were vivid, even to remembering how burned I was about my face. I was surprised to learn from them about my capture.

One of these men was Herr Adolph Heschl, who was seven years old in 1944. He remembered me being brought into town at gunpoint by a hunter. He also remembered my uniform.

Franz Brugner, a newspaper reporter, came to interview me. We sat together at one of the tables, and he asked a number of questions. Our visit was informative for him and renewing of memories for me. I told him the story of our bombing the oil refinery near Vienna; how our bomber was hit by the heavy guns on the ground and struck numerous times by German fighters, and how we had to bail out over Poellau. (Though at the time none of us had any idea where we had landed.) The article appeared in the next day's newspaper.

We met Franz on several other days as he continued to travel with us. He is a tall, handsome man with an optimistic outlook on life, and he is a very good newspaper man. Franz' wife is Traude, a tall, dark-haired, attractive lady, and their son is Simon. Simon found a large section of our plane and brought it to me, along with a photo showing the effects of our bombing the oil refinery.

Herr Zangel came in by himself and sat down with me to tell me about seeing the other members of my crew floating down in their parachutes. They had all bailed out before me and landed in another area. He was about eleven years old at the time.

Another arrival was Burgermeister Franz Winkler. He is the mayor of three small villages and a very nice gentleman. Franz could speak English, and we became close friends. He was with us for several days. Before we left, Franz gave us a book to bring home, *Schonegg Bei Poellau*. This book was about the area where he governed and lived. He wrote these words on the flyleaf: *Dear Mister Dr. Robert Otto. Take this small present for the biggest act of your life. Thankfully, Your mayor, Franz Winkler.*

The next person to arrive was Roman Bruckner. He is a good friend of Josef and they meet often at a gasthaus for a schnapps or glass of wine. Roman also spent several days with us and we got to know him quite well. He is a well educated man in charge of the District Agricultural School, which teaches agricultural subjects, mostly to boys. It is a fascinating place with the main building being an old palace. This is where we had a memorable Thanksgiving meal, much like the ones we have here at home. We all came to like Roman and respect him for his teaching and care of his students.

One day we drove up the mountain to Poellauberg. There we visited with Viktor König and his wife, Sieglinde. They own Bergasthof König, which has been in their family for several generations. It is a beautiful inn and restaurant. They hosted us for a very fine luncheon, and we talked about my former visit to Austria. It was his grandfather, Alexander, who captured me and escorted me down the mountain to the Poellau jailhouse. We sat around the table and talked for quite awhile. It was an interesting time, and he invited us to come back sometime. It would be fun to return and stay a few days with them.

From the mountain we could look down on the village of Poellau and its huge church. We had a fabulous view over the valley, where we could see many small farmhouses and the woods. Everyone was enthralled with the beautiful land-scape. The huge church on the top of this mountain was well worth the trip to visit as well. What a remarkably beauti-ful place!

Wolfgang Brosmann and his photographer were with us several days as they photographed and recorded my visit. Both of these men were well trained in their professions; Wolfgang as a journalist and Gert as a photographer. They are putting together the story of all the American planes that went down in this area. I am looking forward to seeing their completed work.

Peter Mauerhofer is owner of a gasthaus near the woods and field where our plane went down. We had lunch with Peter, then he took us to places where they had found the wreckage of our plane way back in 1944. The engines went down in the woods, as did the cockpit. The engines had land-ed a short distance away in the woods, and the fuselage had crashed in an open field just beyond the woods. There were about ten of us wandering around in these woods, view-ing the areas where different parts had come crashing down. While we were there Randy, my son, dug up a small part from one of the engines. We were amazed he could find something all these years later.

Hermann Schutzenhoefer is the Vice-Governor of the State of Styria. We met him the day we drove to Graz for the presentation of Josef's painting. Hermann was the man in charge, and he gave a speech honoring my presence as representative of the American airmen who went down in their valley. Many were killed during the crashes, and no one knows what happened to the others who survived.

This program was in the headquarters of the Christian Democratic Party, and that is where "The Liberator," (the painting of Harry Moore) is now installed. There was a large crowd and a number of television folks plus several journalists in attendance. We were impressed.

Dr. Herfried and Dr. Susanne Haupt met us during our visit to the Agricultural School. He is a veterinarian, and she is an M.D. Both spoke English so we were able to have some nice talks about veterinary medicine. He works for the government, testing and vaccinating cattle and farm animals. They are both skiers, so we had that in common too, as I am a former ski bum. They were delightful and may come to the U.S. for a visit next year. Hopefully they will be able to come to Washington state. Meanwhile, we keep in touch by e-mail. What a wonderful invention.

We came to love Franz and Gerti Polzhofer like family. Gerti spoke a few words of English but Franz did not, yet somehow we became intertwined with these nice folks who provided us a home-away-from-home.

Franz and Gerti live with Franz' folks in a large, comfortable home equipped with all the modern conveniences. They have a huge garage with two tractors and a car. Franz took Randy and me on a tractor ride that brought back memories of my youth.

Also on the Polzhofer's land is a shed for firewood chips. While we were there they hired a chipper to come in and grind up the wood they had been keeping in preparation for the coming winter. They filled the large shed with wood chips ready to be delivered to the basement room next to their furnace. There is an auger from the furnace to this room that brings the wood right into the furnace. It is a very modern and efficient way of heating their home.

While we were there it was apple picking time. The whole family participated. They used long poles to shake the apples off the trees and then a ladder to climb to the top branches. All of these apples were used to make apple schnapps, a powerful drink that can take your breath away if you are not acquainted with it. It is a favorite of the Austrians.

After we arrived back home the Polzhofers mailed us a letter, saying we would always be welcome to come and stay in their little house. I would be happy to go back at any time.

One of the most interesting and flamboyant men we met was Hans Wiesenhofer, a world famous photographer whose photos have appeared in leading magazines, such as *Life*. He accumulated a fortune during his years as a photographer and was able to return to Poellau and buy a farm from one of his cousins. He tore down the old house and built a beautiful, modern home with all of the accouterments found in homes of the rich and famous. He gave us a tour of his farm, showing the buildings he had built for an art studio and other homes. It was all very impressive. He was a warm gentleman who spoke perfect English and didn't mind bragging about his accomplishments. We appreciated meeting him and joining in a glass of schnapps.

There were other folks we interacted with along the way, for a short visit. The people above were the ones we spent quite some time with, getting to know them and their country. Our hearts were touched by the warmth of the many wonderful people that we now call friends.

Of course the folks who made the biggest impression upon us were Josef, Janice and Louie Schutzenhofer.

Josef Schutzenhofer is no ordinary artist. He is a man with vision and talent, deeply committed to his work, which is about much more than painting a picture. His paintings tell a story that comes from his heart. You can look into the eyes of those he has painted and see joy or anguish, or even bitterness and despair. There is life in his paintings of people.

In 1973 Josef moved to the United States, enrolled at the Cleveland Institute of Art. He ran into financial difficulties, and in 1976 he joined the U.S. Navy. He served until 1980, and was then equipped with the GI Bill and ready to pursue his study of fine arts. By 1987 he had completed undergraduate and graduate degrees from the Maryland Institute College of Art and become a freelance artist. He married Janice in 1997 and moved back to Austria where he lives and paints now.

I am fortunate enough to have four of his paintings hanging on our walls. As I look at them I am drawn back to Austria and the fine people we were privileged to visit. It has been an unforgettable time in my life and the lives of our children.

The purpose of our trip was to help Josef present his painting of Harry Moore to the government of the State of Styria. That painting, "The Liberator," is a memorial to the American airmen who helped free Austria from the grip of Nazi rule. Many of the people in Josef's country lost family and friends during World War II, and some of them blamed the Americans. Josef's intention was to help remedy this bitterness and bring harmony and love back into focus.

Our visit was part of that healing process. I believe it helped those who were struggling with the past to meet someone whom they may have felt bitterness toward. Those of us who were called to serve and ended up dropping bombs were not their enemies, but they felt the impact of our enmity towards the Nazi regime. Certainly, Americans never felt enmity towards the Austrian people. We were doing what we were called into action to do, and we had no choices. (I have to think it was a similar situation for Austrians conscripted into the Nazi's armed forces.)

I am grateful I did not kill anyone in combat. There were times when I had my machine guns trained on an enemy fighter plane, then suddenly that fighter would take a sharp turn and disappear from view.

I am very glad that we had this chance to help return love where there had been hatred and healing where there had been wounds. I believe God was responsible for us getting together, even if we did not realize His presence or actions at the time.

Through the newspaper and television reports the whole nation was made aware of the wonderful memorial that Josef Schutzenhofer created.

He isn't through yet. There are other projects in the works. All we can do is stay tuned in!

Josef, Janet and Louie Schutzenhofer, were the people we first met and came to love in an instant. They were so warm and friendly it would have been impossible not to take them into our own lives. We spent many hours with them, traveling from place to place, dining in various gasthauses and sharing our lives with theirs.

As we prepared to leave to come back home, Janice gave us a beautiful book they had bought for us. It is called *STEI-ER MARK* and is filled with photographs of the State of Styria. It has marvelous photos of the landscape, the homes, the churches and some people. The best part is that the book is written in both German and English, so we can enjoy reading about this picturesque county.

On the flyleaf Janice wrote the following:

"For Dr. Robert Otto and family. This book is a reminder of a remarkable trip taken on by a remarkable man and his family. Your presence has touched the lives of many and possibly even healed many old wounds. You and your family have true friends in Styria now and will always be welcome here. Thank you for coming. Janice, Josef and Louie.

I have traveled in many lands around the world, but have never felt so loved and appreciated as in Styria, Austria. The desire of my heart is to one day return for a longer visit. In the meantime I am awaiting a visit from any of our new friends. We would try our best to host them as comfortably as they have hosted us.

above: Clinic we built, ca. 1978.
L to R Dr. O'Callahan, Dr. Otto. Front: Debbie (receptionist)

below: Treating a sick cow in Kenya
Christian Veterinary Mission, ca. 1985

above:

*Lake Chelan 2007
(l to r standing:)
Robyn Rae,
Robert Randall, Regina
Seated: Robert and Mary
Ann*

right:

*Retirement:
travelling by railroad
from Fairbanks to
Anchorage*

above: (l to r): Hermann Schutzenhoefer (Vice Governor of State of Styria), Josef Schutzenhofer, Robert Otto in front of Josef's painting, "The Liberator." CDP headquarters in Karmeliterplatz, October 2008

below: Robert with new friends, Josef and Janice Schutzenhofer

above: Mr. Schreiner and Robert.
Two old warriors enjoying memories of long ago, October 2008.
(Mr. Schreiner's son Johannes owns Schreiner's Gasthaus.)
Mr. Schreiner passed away in April 2009.

above: "The Liberator" by Josef Schutzenhofer

opposite page, bottom: Robert with the König Family
(r to l) Robert, Viktor König, his wife Sieglinde and Viktor's Moth-
er. They own the Berggasthof König (King's Mountain Inn). Viktor's
grandfather, Alexander, was the man who captured Bob and marched
him down to jail in Poellau in 1944.

• Appendix •
THE SCRIBE'S JOURNAL

My daughter, Regina, kept a daily journal of our trip to Austria, and this may give a better picture than I have been able to portray. Here are her words:

Reggie, Randy and Robyn accompany Dad to Austria for the dedication of "The Liberator" painting by Josef Schutzenhofer to the OVP Styria, and to see where Dad's B-24 Bomber, the *Texarkana Hussy* crashed and Dad was captured.

Tuesday, October 7

We each arrived at Chicago O'Hare about 3:00 p.m. Regina from Dallas, Randy from Anchorage and Robyn from Seattle. We're all together for this big adventure! By the time we'd walked to baggage claim, Dad and Rob's baggage were up. Over to my carousel and there was mine! Then we had to walk over, under, around, across and up (about four miles it seemed) to the hotel shuttle. And onward to the Doubletree O'Hare, provided for us by Paul's Hilton points. (Paul is Regina's husband.)

Lots of laughs sharing the various weird things we brought, breaking into Rob's suitcase and watching Randy iron. Randy suggested we order famous Chicago-style pizza from Giordano's (which took almost one and one half hours to get). It was very good.

Wednesday, October 8

Everyone up, showered and ready for breakfast. Down to the hotel restaurant where they tried to push the $15.95 buffet, but we opted for less food.

Took the shuttle back to the airport. Through security with no problems and we boarded LH435 for a 2:10 departure aboard an A340-600.

The seating was very tight, but we did get to sit together-four across in the center area. Each seat had its own TV screen with nine movie choices. We all had chicken dinner with rice and an apple strudel.

Only Randy was able to get any sleep (being a pilot for Alaska Airlines he has lots of experience deadheading.) A poor little two year old baby in the row in front of us cried the better part of our eight hour flight. The plane was hot. The restrooms were downstairs.

Most of the flight was smooth. We arrived in very foggy Munich at 5:30 AM.

Thursday, October 9

Deplaned. We had to go through passport control and back through security (quite a walk) to get our gate for Austrian 220 to Vienna. Two hours to wait before boarding. Heavy fog delayed our flight, but we finally arrived, four exhausted travelers, in Vienna.

Our baggage was waiting and so were Josef and Janice Schutzenhofer, holding an "Otto Family" sign. No customs or passport control. Josef and Janice seemed as excited as little kids to see us. We hopped into their VW bus and headed downtown for a tour.

Stopped at their favorite Viennese coffeehouse, Cafe Sperl. Dad and I shared apfelstrudel—yum! We dropped Rob and Janice off at the Naschmarkt. The rest of us went to Esterhazypark to see one of the World War II flak towers. Flak is an acronym for Fliegerabwehrkanone, meaning anti-aircraft gun. In Vienna three pairs of towers were constructed by German troops during 1943 and 1944 forming a defensive triangle centered on the city's great cathedral, the Stephansdom. Each pair consisted of a large, heavily gunned attack tower (Gefechtsturm) and a smaller communications tower (Leitturm). They were designed by Friedrich Tamms, the Father of the Autobahn. Made of steel reinforced concrete, the walls are 8-12 feet thick and range from 137-166 feet high.

Flak towers were also built in Berlin and Hamburg, but only the Vienna towers remain. The one in Esterhazypark was a Leitturm and now houses an aquarium.

We met back at the Naschmarkt where we saw several art-deco style buildings. Then we took the scenic route to Poellau.

Pulled into the driveway of the gasthaus where we are staying and were immediately met by our hostess Gerti and her in-laws the Polshofers. Sweet people. No English.

Our little house has two bedrooms, a banquette and table, kitchen, bathroom and a porcelain stove for heat. Cute and cozy.

We took a quick nap before heading to Gasthaus Schreiner for dinner. The owners and chef, Johannes and Renate, opened just for our dinner and a get-together. Randy had Grosser beer and homemade sausage. Rob and I had weinerschnitzel. Dad had pumpkin soup and lamb chops. (Yum) Plus, Randy, Rob and I had delicious garlic soup! We were joined by Josef, Janice and their son Louie.

After dinner the first guest arrived—Herr Adolf Heschl. (Josef calls him Herr Heschl because he won't call anyone

Adolf.) He was seven years old and remembered Dad being brought into town at gunpoint by the hunter who found him after he landed. He recalled the burns on Dad's face, which triggered Dad's memory of looking into the puddles along the way trying to see his burns. Herr Herschl also remembers Dad's blue uniform.

Johannes's Schreiner's dad arrived next, eager to try out his English! The Inn has been in his family for three generations. It was rebuilt in 1794 after being destroyed by fire. He had been drafted into the German army and served on the Russian front near the Black Sea. He was proud to say, "Two old war veterans 85 and 86 years old!"

Soon the reporter, Franz Brugner, came in to interview Dad and take pictures for an article in *Keline Zeitung.*

The table was filling up. Wine was brought in—a bottle of sturm, a slightly fermented grape juice, which Randy really liked! It's available about three weeks a year.

Herr Zangl, who was about eleven years old at the time, told Dad he saw the other survivors from his plane as they parachuted into the valley.

Several other Poellauers stopped in to meet Dad, including Burgermeister Franz Winkler of Schonegg and Roman Bruckner, the head of Landwirtschaftschule- the district agricultural school. They have all been warm and friendly, very interested in Dad and his story. It seems everyone in the Poellau valley knows the Americans are here!

Josef said the Austrians were polarized by the German invasion. Very poor economic conditions following World War I had made Austria a prime target for Hitler. Many Austrians saw him as a rescuer. And by the time Dad arrived, heavy resentment toward Americans existed because of the bombing. There still exists, among a few people, anger towards America because of the loss of portions of Austria when it was partitioned by the Allies at the end of the war. Josef said Austria still receives money from the Marshall Plan, which was designed to return economic stability and reconstruct the country.

Janice took Dad, Rob and me back to our little house. Randy stayed at the gasthaus for conversation. (He could understand and speak some German having studied some 30 years ago in college.) The fire had been stoked in the porcelain stove by our gracious hosts so it was quite warm! And we were ready for sleep.

Friday, October 10

Up about seven AM. Randy cooked bacon and omelet with ingredients Janice had provided. She brought over fresh rolls from the backerei and we also had Brie with Josef's Mother's homemade apricot and red currant jams.

It's a beautiful clear morning! Josef and Janice stayed for coffee. Josef brought all of his research pictures, MPERs (Missing Persons Evaluation Report) from the government and maps of the area. He showed us on the map exactly where Dad's plane landed and where Dad was captured as well as the other three planes. Dad gave Josef his B-24 cap.

We piled into Josef's van, went into Poellau and parked at the castle where Josef's studio is located. We visited the Poellauer church, built about 1100 AD. A magnificent cathedral – the largest building in town, by far.

Stopped at the gift shop then walked through the town square to Konditorei Ebner to have coffee and pastries.

Back into the van and on to Graz, about 50 km away. The scenery along the way was beautiful—hilly farmland, trees loaded with apples ready to pick, and corn fields ready for harvest for the pigs of southern Styria. We arrived in Graz about noon. We saw the hospital where Dad was taken by the Germans. Josef dropped us off at the Freiheitsplatz while he parked the van. We walked through the shopping area, across the tram tracks and met him at the Rathaus in Hauptplatz. From there we walked to Glickenspielplatz and had lunch at Altmune Gasthaus. Very pleasant al fresco dining. Randy had sour cream soup and Big Bean salad with pumpkin seed oil dressing. Dad had buckwheat soup. Rob and I had huge frankfurters with pomme frites. Some beer, apple juice (apfelsaft) and Coke.

Took the lift to the top—Schlossbergstallen, a mountain in the center of Old Town Graz. It is honeycombed with caves where the people of Graz hid during air raids in World War II. We looked over the famous red-roofed city, which has been designated as a world cultural site.

Hervig Holler, a reporter, met us at the top to interview Dad for an upcoming article. He walked down the mountain with us as we headed toward the Christian Democratic Party Hq (OVP) in Karmeliterplatz for the presentation of the painting. Invitations had been sent to many area officials. A film crew from ORF filmed the event (which was shown on national Austrian TV this evening).

Hermann Schutzenhoefer, the Vice-Governor of Styria, gave a lovely speech honoring Dad for his role in helping to liberate Austria. He spoke about Josef's role in pulling all this together. He encouraged the Austrians to keep this perspective of liberation. Josef spoke about his vision for the painting and how he wasn't a reconciler but wanted respect for those who liberated Austria from the Nazis. He made a PowerPoint™ presentation explaining the vision and development of the painting. A nice reception followed. We visited with a pleasant young councilman from Beirbaum. Roman Bruckner and Burgermeister Winkler were there too.

After the reception, we walked back to the van, parked about one half mile away, outside the gate. Randy bought some roasted chestnuts. Everyone was very tired on the drive back to Poellau, as the sun set. Seeing the lighted Poellauberg church sitting high on the hill, we knew we were near our little house.

As soon as we turned into the driveway, the lights came on at Polshofers and over came Franz and Gerti with schnapps for everyone. Back and forth Franz went, bringing more types for us to try—apricot, cherry, plum, pear and a blueberry liqueur! Yikes! Schnapps is the national liqueur of Austria. Locally made, it contains a minimum of 32% alcohol and up to 80%. Potent stuff. Burns all the way down and then some ... must be an acquired taste which we haven't acquired and all the Austrians have.

Randy is a trooper—finishing all our glasses for us. Rob and I hurriedly cut up our sandwich meat-bologna, salami, and ham, swiss cheese, apples, oranges, fresh bread and soon we had a real party going.

After everyone left, we had a lengthy family chat. Went to bed about 1:30.

Saturday October 11

Up early. Showered. Rob fried bacon and eggs for herself, Janice and Dad. Randy went to Josef's to use the computer.

We took photos of Franz harvesting apples by shaking the trees—very picturesque.

Rob, Janice and I went to town to shop. "Grusse Gut," from all the shop owners. Loosely translated to, "good health" "Greetings." We saw all the shops, really enjoyed the Blumen (flower shop) which had very interesting, creative arrangements. Rob bought a scarf and a cross for Mom and several gifts for the people at work. Janice got some deer sausage for us to try at the farmer's market.

While we were in town, Dad, Randy and Josef drove by the deer farm and met up with the film crew—Wolfgang Brosmann and his cameraman Gert, who are making a documentary of all the planes that crashed in the Hartberg district. They were already at Herr Grasser's house. They all drove on to Poellauberg where we met up with them. We met Herr Viktor König and his wife, Sieglinde who own Berggasthof König (King's Mountain Inn). This inn was built in 1708. The König family took over in 1893 and this is the fifth generation of König's to run it. After a short interview we learned that Viktor's grandfather, Alexander, was the hunter who captured Dad when he landed. They hosted us for a lively lunch.

Randy and I had mushroom soup. Rob and Janice had firttatensupe – with crepe-like pancakes in a clear broth. Randy and Janice had salads with sheep cheese squares fried with sesame seeds. Rob, Dad and I thought we were sharing one potato with cheese and bacon that turned out to be one potato each – a baked potato with pesto, bacon, garlic and sour cream. It was unique and delicious.

A quick stop at the gift shop gave Dad the opportunity to buy a blue tractor set mounted on a board which read

"Good enough to start again." Rob and I bought some porcelain dishes.

From there we followed Herr Grosser and the camera crew on a wild goose chase. He thought he remembered where he saw Dad land, but it was actually the site of a German pilot's landing. That didn't stop us! The family who owned the land (and their neighbors who showed up to meet "the Americans") brought out some schnapps and we all toasted, "Prosit!" Gert said he thought they were brewing their own moonshine.

An hour later we headed back to Poellauberg to pick up Janice's car. She left to get Louie and stop at the grocery store while the rest of us took off for Gasthaus Mauerhof. Once there, Simon Brugner arrived with his photos. He also brought Dad a piece of the cowling he'd found at the crash site.

A table was set up outside where Herr Brosmann and Dad sat down for a long interview. As cars and tractors drove by, questions were asked and answered, film was changed. We sat in the yard of Gasthaus Mauerhof, across the road from the *Texarkana Hussy*'s crash site, as Dad relived the moments that profoundly altered his life.

Herr Mauerhof came out and described his view. He was working under a tree as he heard the plane's engines faltering. He saw the parachutes open as the crew escaped the burning aircraft. As he watched them gently float down, it appeared to him as though the plane itself was spiraling directly toward his family's home. Suddenly the plane exploded and he ran for safety. When he realized the plane's pieces had landed in the nearby field, he ran to the site. Less than one kilometer away from his house, his first view was of the fuselage. He looked around and found an engine about 100 yards away.

Later, this fifteen year old boy discovered the cockpit, with the burned remains of nose-gunner Earl Sullivan and copilot Ken Reed.

Today a young forest has grown over the crash site, re-claiming the land. A peaceful meadow hides the scars of the fuselage. The plane is no longer there. It was taken in pieces by nearby farmers, cut up and used for repairs to their build-ings.

The graves that temporarily housed Ken Reed and Earl Sullivan have been removed and their remains returned home. Only memories remain. For a strong 79 year old farmer and gasthaus owner, the memories are vivid.

For a great grandfather from America, the memories are harder to coax awake. But the two heart-bypass patients opened those hearts to each other in the woods of Poellau, a fitting conclusion to two men's lives inexorably joined sixty four years ago.

Following the interviews, the Mauerhofs shared a sim-ple workman's lunch with us—goulash soup and brot. With wine, of course. And always schnapps to end the meal. Herr Mauerhof was a generous host, and Herr Winkler paid.

Some people walked to the crash site. Josef drove Dad. We saw the meadow where the fuselage landed, then we walked into the woods. Randy climbed into the depression where one engine crashed down. Under the carpet of mulch he dug around and found two pieces of the engine. One may have been a piston cover and the other some sort of fuel line. We walked uphill, quarter of a mile, to where the cockpit had landed. The area was fairly large where airplane pieces littered the ground following the explosion.

Only a large mound marks the spot where the cockpit rested. We returned to the gasthaus where we saw several colorful hot air balloons floating overhead.

We were accompanied on this journey into the past by Herr Mauerhof, Simon Brugner, Schonegg Burgermeister Franz Winkler, Roman Bruckner, the film crew of Wolfgang Brosmann and Gert, and Josef & Janice Schutzenhofer.

We returned to our little house to rest and sample some fresh baked cakes from Gerti before the Poellau reception at Gasthaus Schreiner. At Johannes and Renate's the guests included Franz Winkler, Roman Bruckner, Ernst the wood-worker, two teachers from Louie's school and Wolfgang Brosmann. Josef made a PowerPoint™ presentation, more detailed than the one in Graz and with English translation.

Hannas and Renate made a light dinner of air-dried ham, grated horseradish and brot for us. Out came the beer, wine and the ever present schnapps. We came home to a warm cozy house and got a good night's sleep.

Sunday, October 12

A BIG day in store for us.

First—it's TRACTOR DAY for Dad and Randy. Franz took them for a ride on his oldest tractor. They were up and gone by 8:00. Franz brought Dad a warm coat, a blanket, hat with flaps and a rope to tie him down. They sat on seats mounted above the wheels and went to the deer farm, then to Franz's great aunt's house. She held Dad's hand and gazed into his eyes for a long time, then talked to him in German. It seemed she was very appreciative of Dad's war effort.

All the people we have met have been incredibly gracious, warm and hospitable. So many are simple farmers, living simple lives on the same farms for generations. Poellau valley is almost a throwback to an earlier time, a slower pace of living, always time to talk. The town of Poellau has about 2,100 people. Poellauberg, high on the mountaintop, has about 2,250 and the whole valley totals about 7,000.

The roads through the hills weren't paved until the 1980s. This valley is part of the Hartberg district, one of sixteen districts in Styria. The entire state is called Styria. (Steiermark in German) and is called "The Green Heart of Austria." It is the second biggest state in Austria. The capitol is Graz. The total population of Styria is about 1.2 million. About 56% of Styria is forested and is becoming more forested as unused farmland is reclaimed.

Several people talked to us about life in Poellau during the war. The area was so isolated—no radio communication, no paved roads. They worked their farms, unaware of world events. Then the Germans came to occupy the towns and take many men to serve in the German army on the Russian Front. Josef told us there was very little resistance in the valley. (In Hartberg twenty-nine resisters were hung by the SS just two days before the war ended, on May 8, 1945.)

The locals watched huge formations of American bombers flying high overhead, back and forth on their bombing runs to Moosbeirbaum Oil Refinery, northwest of Vienna, and other points. They left large contrails in their wake.

When the Germans left, the Russians came. Still they worked their farms with whatever men hadn't been conscripted to serve in the German army. The Jews had all been taken away. Today there are no Jews in the area. The people are almost all Catholic. In the Hartberg district of 67,000 there are only 400 Protestants (mostly Lutheran). Janice, married to a local, Josef, has been here for seventeen years and is still considered an outsider.

Back on the tractor. Franz was very concerned about Dad and kept him warm on this very cool, brisk October morn. When they stopped, he tenderly lifted Dad down. Franz speaks no English yet he communicated well. He's a gentle, soft spoken Poellauer who owns a small farm but makes his living selling and installing specialty glass like 10,000 pieces for the Poellau church. He raises a special kind of bull as an incentive from the European Union to improve the meat quality, He also grows apples to make apple juice and apple schnapps. Gerti, his wife, speaks some English shyly. She works in the Hartberg Hospital as a cleaner. They have two children.

Randy and Dad returned from their big adventure. We had granola bars and bananas for breakfast. Josef brought over the Kleine Zeitung Sunday paper with Franz Brugner's article about Dad, entitled, "After sixty four years, back to the crash site." Josef translated for us.

After a relaxing morning, we left in Josef's van to take the scenic route (his preferred travel route) to Hartberg, over the mountain. We stopped for photos on the backside of Poellauberg.

We were by Director Roman Bruckner greeted upon arrival at the Landwirtshaftschule Kirchberg . Originally a castle built in 1130, it was placed in the National Trust several years ago. The agricultural school is for boys ages 14 -18 years old and some girls attend too, who plan to work in the agricultural field. They have a full course of study including religion, animal husbandry, bee-keeping, farm production and of course schnapps production.

Janice, Josef's sister, Waltraud, and Susie Haupt had been cooking the feast since 8:00 a.m. They served appetizers including lox puffs, bacon puffs, vegetables with dips, prosciutto with tomato and cucumber, celery with cream cheese and chives, dark bread squares with a green paste (yummy), deviled eggs, and red peppers with paprika cream cheese. Susie made a drink with peach nectar and peach schnapps which was very good and made schnapps much more palatable.

Roman took us on a tour of the school. There are 160 students currently enrolled. 140 stay in dorms all week and go home on the weekends. Twenty commute to school. They receive four meals a day—breakfast at 6:00, repast at 9:00, dinner at 12:00 and supper at 6:00. They are responsible for taking care of all the animals as well as the vegetable garden. The school is fairly self-sustaining. Chickens for eggs, pigs and cows for slaughter and milk. There are greenhouses as well as gardens for vegetables. There is a bee house for honey. They make their own apple juice, wine and schnapps, which they sell at the farmer's market. They build pens and buildings on the property which has a carpentry shop, metal shop and machine shop. They are raising cattle as an experimental program to create a "dual" cow—good for milk and for meat.

Currently they have Holsteins and Simmentals. Randy took a Lambourgini tractor for a drive. We stopped by Roman's office and saw a painting Josef had done. Roman was the schnapps instructor for eight years, during which the school won eight schnapps championships, of which he is very proud. So, of course, we ended the tour with a glass of schnapps to toast Schnappsbrenner Roman.

We returned to the teachers' dining room where tables were set for dinner. Janice had prepared two turkeys, mashed potatoes and gravy, stuffing, carrots with broccoli, Brussels sprouts, and a rolled bread cube dish. We had wine made by the school. Desserts included an orange cream cake, made by Elizabeth, Roman's wife, a chocolate granache cake from the Brosmann family and Janice's mini pumpkin tarts.

Also attending the dinner were Herfried and Susie Haupt (he is the state veterinarian for Hartberg district and teaches special classes at the school; she is a medical doctor.) Roman's wife Lisl (Elizabeth) (is also a medical doctor) and their son and daughter plus a friend of the family; Burgermeister Franz Winkler, Wolfgang Brosmann with his wife and three children; Franz and Traude Brugner with their sons, Simon and Philip and their girlfriends, who all attend the university in Vienna.

Toasts were made to the good cooks, to Josef, to Roman and to Dad. Dad also made a toast thanking everyone for making this the best trip of his life. Janice wanted everyone to enjoy an American Thanksgiving dinner. We all loved the food. We have much to be thankful for.

In Austria they have a day of Thanksgiving in early October, a religious event to celebrate the harvest. They have parades of decorated wagons displaying the bounty of the harvest. No meal involved (but probably schnapps).

It was a fun, educational and special day. Roman summed it up best when he said the castle was hated because the peasants had to pay taxes to the owners. Now the castle gives back to the land through educating the farmers' families. In the same way, he said, Austria was the enemy of Dad's country and now Dad comes to Austria as a friend.

Being full of turkey and tryptophan, we were all tired and glad to see our house for another good night's sleep in a cozy cottage with a freshly stoked fire.

Monday, October 13

We started the day with a light snack of bananas, local pears, apple juice and coffee. Josef took us to see his art studio.

He's an amazing artist, working in oils with a special shaving technique to make the paint smooth on the canvas. He also works in watercolors. He does considerable contract work, especially for auto makers, making detailed artwork of concept cars, variable steering mechanisms and some heavy equipment. He was commissioned to paint the President of Austria. His famous worker paintings on wood were done for a large clothing manufacturer. He likes to watercolor while on vacation, especially in Croatia.

Josef's personality is reflected through his subtle sarcasm as in his paintings of unpopular men shown with the Presidential colors in the background—somewhat of a rebellious political thinker. Sometimes his views get him on the opposite side of politicos.. (Like the Burgermeister of Poellau).

We would never have known how well respected his work is in Austria from him—he's very self-deprecating. We heard the stories from his many friends we met.

We picked up Janice on the way to Vorau, the town where the hospital she works in is located. Our first stop was Augustiner Chorherrenstift Vodrau, a monastery built in 1163, along with a very ornate church. The grounds were very nice. It houses a home economics school as well as an artist's studio. Behind the walls are several open courtyards. We didn't stay long. The restaurant wasn't open because it is Monday. So we drove through town and up a hill to a local gasthaus, Brenner Wirt. They had no hot food because it is more like a pub, a local hangout. Rob and I shared an air-dried ham and cheese platter. Dad had smoked trout. Randy had a ham sausage. They were all good. Janice had a delicious cut meat salad, similar to bologna with pumpkin seed oil. We all shared bites. Josef ate the big beans. Randy had some of the local sturm. For dessert, we all shared a piece of chocolate cake warmed with chocolate sauce and whipped cream. We returned to the house for a nap

Josef picked us up and we headed for Hans Wiesenhofer's ultra modern home on the opposite side of the valley. Hans is a world-famous Time/Life photographer who returned to Poellau valley when his cousin decided to sell the family farm. Hans bought it, razed the family home and built a sleek, flat-roofed home with all modern conveniences, enormous triple pane windows, and solar-like heat in the slate floor. After a glass of wine on the patio, he took us inside to see his handiwork: walnut two inch thick stairs, four by eight foot table made out of a single piece of wood, ten foot movable shutters for the windows to keep the cold out.

Hans walked with us down his cobbled brick drive, past two old farmhouses and his remodeled barn which is now an enormous studio, and through a field to an outbuilding which used the aluminum sheet metal from Harry Moore's plane for the roof repair. Hans has ten hectares which have pear trees and apple trees. His neighbor, who is the best pear schnapps producer in Styria, using Hans' pears, stopped by. It takes thirty years for these pear trees to begin producing usable fruit. Hans said that to buy farm land, you have to farm it. So he planted new trees to replace the ones his cousins had let die and now his neighbor does the harvesting. Hans called himself a "prostitute" because he photographs for money while Josef is the true artist. But he was quick to mention the home he built and the improvements to the farm have cost him between three and four million euros, so his prostitution has been profitable.

From there we went next door (which was down the hill, across the stream, around the bend, past several homes and up the hill) to the "old Dieterbauer place" where the Pottler family has lived for seventy years. Josef, the young farmer, is the man who allowed Josef to place the delta marker memorial on his property pointing to the location where Harry Moore's plane crashed. He showed us several pieces of Moore's plane which had been salvaged. When the plane crashed in February 1944, it is believed only three survived. Several bodies weren't discovered until spring when the stench bothered the animals. The local people wanted the bodies buried in Poellau. The elder Pottler insisted they be buried in the woods nearby. They were removed and returned home after the war.

Josef's painting, "The Liberator," features his impression of what Harry Moore looked like, as he was unable to discover any photos. The names of the Ramp Tramp crew are inscribed on the painting and are also on the delta marker.

Herr Reiterer, a neighbor who was thirteen years old at the time, saw Dad's plane crash. Dressed in his best Styrian wear and hat, he was very talkative. He said a bomb dropped from an Allied plane landed on his family's house and killed his mother. We hope we convinced him it wasn't Dad's plane: they had already dropped their payload over the target area.

Josef Pottler's Aunt Appalonia remembered the day Harry Moore's plane crashed. She was in Poellau and thought the plane had hit their home. She was terrified. A feisty, tiny woman who walks with ski poles and hiking boots around the farm, she is nearly deaf from a stroke, but it hasn't slowed her down. She loves to sing. She and her brother sang together at weddings when they were growing up. She shared an Austrian folk song about tears falling on flowers. She loves poetry and recited a poem for us. Without a word of English, she shared her joie de vivre with all of us and we are the better for having met her.

We were invited into the Pottler home for drinks similar to wine spritzers. Then plates of cookies were brought out. They had been made for baby Daniel's baptism the day before. There are three children, including two daughters about 18 months and four years old, in this sweet family. They keep a "traditional" farm according to Roman, who came by after work. It was a very nice ending to a very special week.

What an incredible opportunity we had—to be welcomed into so many Austrian homes, to meet so many Poellau valley families, to share a drink, some food and many laughs— to bind us together.

How different for Dad these days have been from his original visit to this valley on June 26, 1944, when scared and angry farmers saw seven parachutes float onto their farmlands as a fiery plane crash resounded through the hills. Lives were changed on that day—the life of a young Idaho man who was marched into Poellau at gunpoint, burned about his upper body; taken to a Graz hospital for treatment; loaded like cattle onto a train for Gros Tychow, Poland and Stalag Luft IV; and finally survived a 500-mile march around the German countryside before his liberation. And the lives of simple farm folk, isolated from the war except for the German soldiers occupying their towns, until four Allied planes crashed into their valley, a harsh reminder they were indeed at war. In many ways these were the most memorable moments of their lives. Sixty four years later they still recall, in vivid detail, the sights and sounds that assailed this quiet land. They remember a young burned American airman.

Now they have been reacquainted, sharing stories and schnapps, mirth and memories. So many years have passed—from one end of life to the other. Both have been liberated from their pasts as this week has passed by. And so Josef's dream of liberation has come to fruition.

These people have left footprints on our hearts and we will never be the same. I hope we have done the same for them.

Tuesday, October 14

Time to say good bye to precious Janice, who worked so hard behind the scenes to make our trip so special. We were able to say goodbye also to Gerti and her inlaws. A little sad but packed and ready, we boarded Josef's van for the last time and headed towards Vienna. For the first time since we landed, the weather was overcast and gloomy—a fitting reminder that we didn't want to leave.

He dropped us off at the Vienna Hilton Stadtpark where we said our final goodbyes to a remarkable and tenacious man, Josef Schutzenhofer, whom we now call friend.

Check in was smooth. They put us in two rooms on the Executive floor which gave us the benefit of the Executive Lounge. Randy had some coffee, we had juice and coke and some cookies. Randy checked with concierge who directed us to a restaurant for our final real Austrian lunch. We headed out of the hotel and wandered our way to lunch, stopping at several shops, making some last minute purchases, particularly Pashminas, as we headed up Wollzeile to our restaurant Figlmuller, on a side alley off the main road. They promote themselves as having the best Schnitzel in Vienna so we decided to try it. Our waiter suggested we order one half schnitzels and he was correct. They were huge—covering our plates and so tender and delicious. We added their potato-field salad with Styrian pumpkin seed oil dressing which was also fantastic. Yum-o.

After our wonderful repast, we needed to walk it off so we headed to St. Stephens Square and the enormous old cathedral which stands in the center of Vienna. Construction began in 1147 and has both Romanesque and Gothic influences. During World War II St. Stephens Cathedral was saved from intentional destruction at the hands of retreating German forces when Captain Gerhard Klinkicht disregarded orders from the city commandant, Sepp Dietrich, to "fire a hundred shells and leave it in just debris and ashes." On April 12, 1945, however, fires from nearby shops—started by civilian plunderers as Russian troops entered the city— were carried to the cathedral by wind, severely damaging the roof and causing it to collapse. Fortunately, protective brick shells built around the pulpit, Frederick III's tomb, and other treasures, minimized damage to the most valuable artworks. The beautifully carved 1487 Rollinger choir stalls, however, could not be saved. Rebuilding began immediately, with a limited reopening on 12 December 1948 and a full reopening on 23 April 1952. The towers stand 445 feet tall and no building in Vienna can be taller than they are.

From there we watched some street performers and walked part way down Kartnerstrasse, turning onto Johannesgasse to the Ring. Randy checked out the bicycles which are for rent around town. We walked through Stadtpark, past the Johann Strauss statue and back to our hotel.

Dad and Rob rested in the lobby while Randy and I went to Starbuck's and brought back a mocha for Dad. They went up to our rooms while Randy and I looked for the CAT Terminal. We couldn't find it so we talked to a taxi driver and found out it wouldn't cost much more to take a taxi to the airport. We walked back up Wollzeile and bought Dad a sweater he liked, then returned to the hotel and had a "snack" in the Executive Lounge—shrimp, sausage rolls, several desserts and other goodies, Just enough dinner. It was a quiet and restful evening and we all went to bed early.

Wednesday, October 15

Up early, dressed and packed. We went to the Executive Lounge for some breakfast, when it opened at 6 AM, then down to the lobby and got a taxi—which cost more than we were told. We figured out that we could have saved money by going out the other door to a different taxi stand. Oh well!

Checked into the Vienna airport to catch our flight to Munich where we connected to our Chicago flight. Things went fairly smoothly at the airport as far as check-in and getting the wheelchair which enabled us to get through security easily. Rob wandered off to look at the shops. Dad and Randy had a coffee. The only real problem on the whole trip was trying to get early boarding on the flight to Chicago. An inept attendant failed to check us in at the gate and we ended up being among the last to board ... after a little meltdown by me and some tough talk by Rob. But, we made it.

Dad's TV didn't work so I traded him places and sat with Randy. We had a good lunch and everyone was quiet—writing, reading, sleeping watching movies. The flight was a little bumpy in places but otherwise uneventful. It was cold and rainy when we arrived in Chicago. Took a long time to get our luggage and through security but we did it. Randy walked us out and waited with us until the hotel shuttle arrived. Then he went back in and caught a flight to Anchorage. That's a lot of flying!

I know he is used to being on planes but I am sure glad it wasn't us getting on another flight after all those hours crossing the Atlantic. Ciao, brother!!!

Dad, Rob and I went to the Renaissance Suites and checked in to our little suite. We had two double beds, black-out curtains, and a nice sitting area. Went to the hotel's restaurant for a bite of dinner before falling into bed. We were sound asleep by 8:00 p.m.

We all woke up about 3:00 a.m.—just the time Randy's flight was landing in Anchorage. But, we were able to get back to sleep

Thursday October 16

We indulged ourselves at the breakfast buffet in the hotel restaurant before heading to O'Hare.

We got ourselves all checked in through the kiosks, the wheelchair arrived and we breezed through security. Our gates were near each other so we sat together waiting for the

Seattle flight which left first. Finally it was time for Dad and Rob to board.

It was hard to say goodbye having shared a once-in-a-life-time experience which bonded us in new and deeper ways. We came to understand each other better. We were able to share in the events which honored our father so well. We walked in places where Dad had walked and saw places with him for the first time. We met people who had seen our Father before we were ever born.

I can see that goodbyes will always hurt. I know that all the photos we took will never replace being in the moment there. And the truth is that heroes too often go unsung.

Thank you Daddy, for enabling us to share this journey with you.

I end with two quotes:

*"I cannot say good-bye to those whom I have grown to love,
for the memories we have made will last a lifetime and
never know a good-bye."*
(unknown)

*"Don't cry because it's over.
Smile because it happened."*
(Dr. Seuss)

· Afterword ·
REFLECTIONS

The wonder of it all! Someone has been in charge of my life since day one. Most of the time I thought I was in charge. *Not so!* God has been in charge and I am forever grateful! As I look back and think of all the things I have been through and how my life has been spared, I have to believe it was because of Someone greater than I. Someone who loves me with an unending love.

For example, when I was seventeen a big tractor tipped over on me. A local tractor dealer had brought a new model for my Dad to try. It was set up so the rear wheels could be extended outward or adjusted inward to make it narrower. The wheels were set close to the body of the tractor and as I was driving around a corner the tractor tipped over right on top of me. I couldn't move. Fortunately, one of my brothers and another man were busy working right in this area. They rushed over and with super human strength were able to tip the tractor back into an upright position, freeing me and allowing me to get up. I was bruised but nothing broken. Was it happenstance that those two men were right there and able to push that heavy machinery upright? I don't think so.

Then there was another occasion when I was driving along with my small son and another car ran a stop sign and crashed into the driver's side door. Neither one of us was seriously injured. It was a lesson to remember to be especially careful and watchful as you drive.

The time when I had to bail out of our B-24 bomber over Austria when it was on fire was another miracle. The fire was rushing down the inside of the plane with inferno force and I was trying to get out of my turret and make my way to the escape hatch. Just in time I jumped out, but I had my flak vest on over my parachute and there was no way I could pull the cord and expect the parachute to open. Miraculously, while falling fast and somersaulting at the same time, I was able to remove the flak vest and pull the cord on the parachute. What a wonderful feeling that was when the chute opened and I floated quietly down. It must have been only a few seconds after I escaped from the plane that I saw it explode in mid air. Did Someone have a hand on me? I believe so. Two of our crew were killed, either by gunfire or during the crash. No one knew.

Was it circumstances or a miracle that sixty-four years later I was able to participate in a ceremony honoring American airmen in Austria? This all came about, not by anything I was doing. In fact, I hadn't thought about the war in a long, long time. Suddenly, I was jolted back to that time by getting in touch with a wonderful artist in Austria. Was this just a lucky meeting or was it ordered by a Higher Order? I believe God had His hand on my life since the night I surrendered my life to Him in that little Baptist Church at the age of seventeen. Of course He had his hand on me even before that for the Bible says God knew us, even in our mother's womb. But, it wasn't until that night in a revival meeting that He became real to me. That night my life was changed. I wasn't always faithful to God but He was always faithful to me and my life has been good because of that.

Jesus said, "I will never leave you, nor forsake you." That has been true for me all of my life. Now here I am in the sunset years, still enjoying and believing even better things will take place. Like getting this story published, that my family may have good memories of this old man. I know my two daughters do, for they have written and told me, not too long ago.

The older daughter:

My Dad is a great Dad. He is an unusual Dad. In fact, he is an outstanding Dad. He is a Godly Dad. He is an honest, ethical and wise Dad. He is known across Christendom as a Christian servant.

But, as strange is it may seem, to me he is just Dad. His wisdom seems to be a bottomless resource and how often I've called upon it! His humor is as much a tool in his arsenal of relating to people as it is a simply joyous part of his life. And how much I've benefited from it!

He probably has his faults, but I am not aware of them— don't remember them. The goodness of the man outweighs anything he might have done that was somehow off-kilter. Maybe I just take him for granted but I don't mean to. He's always been there for me.

What really makes a good Dad? A Dad that you could honor, as the Bible commands? A dad who lives an exemplary life of godly fear, yet fears no man? What makes a mere man into a more than a mere Dad?

To me, the answer is simple. It's found in 2 Corinthians 5. He is reconciled to God. And he lives a life that reflects that reconciliation, a life that honors the heavenly Father. He helps me SEE God in His creation, in His people, in His love. He helps me see how God intends for us to live in relationship with Him. I'm thankful to have a Dad like that. And how much I love him! How blessed I am.

The younger daughter:

Sitting in church this morning made me realize I've never told you how proud I am of you or of being your daughter.

When you got a standing ovation and people kept clapping I was so proud of you. Not only for being a war hero but for being a man of God filled with courage, honor, integrity and faithfulness.

I love you with all of my heart and I'm so honored to be your daughter.

Thank you for being such an example to me of God's love. My love of God, my strength, and my perseverance all come from the examples you've set for me. Many times in my life I've felt like quitting but I always hear my Dad telling me to "hang in there" and "never give up. God's in control."

Thanks Dad for always being there for me and being such a great friend.

I cherish all our memories and good times we've shared. Thanks for loving me when I didn't deserve it and for always brightening my days with your smile.

Forever my love.

My son hasn't written anything like these two notes, so I can't include one here, but I know how much he loves me. Whenever we part we always say, "I love you," and I know it comes from his heart. He is a good man.

This is why it was such a joy to have all three of our children with me on the journey to Austria. Our family is strong in our love for one another and for our Lord Jesus Christ who is "The Alpha and Omega, The Beginning and the End."

We have had our ups and downs. There were times when we thought God had abandoned us.

1. There was the time when the first doctor I worked for after graduation promised me a future and a partnership. We settled in, bought our first home for the family. Not long after, when things got tough, I was let go and the job and the future partnership vanished, to say nothing of the new house to pay for. I was still God's and didn't know I still had much to learn. It wasn't time to settle down. He gave me a new job at better pay, rented our home and sent us off on a new adventure.

2. We moved to Manhattan, Kansas and I landed a staff job at the College of Veterinary Medicine in Kansas State University. They had promised me, if I worked as a large animal clinician training the students and taking the senior class members out on farm calls, they would give me time to work on an advanced degree toward a future in the world of academia. It turned out they just wanted a clinician and the time for a degree didn't come forth. No point in staying here. But, God had another plan! He sent us out on a new job for Hill Packing Company, with a company car, expense account, and back into our own home in the Pacific Northwest.

3. After we built the clinic and business began to prosper, we began to build a nest egg for the future. Along with three other veterinarians, we bought nine acres of undeveloped land and built a business park with five large buildings. At one point, one of our tenants decided to sue us for some imagined shortcomings.

Had we lost the case, all four us would have lost it all—clinics, homes and everything. The case dragged on for weeks and our partners, who had more to lose than we, were under a lot of stress. But, we had peace! We didn't lose the case but were exonerated, and He blessed us for being faithful.

There were other times of disappointment, but God was always faithful to turn our human sidetracks and wrong turns to good. That's how much He loves us. To God be the glory.

My life has been a full one. The regrets I have are few. The love, joy and peace I have are unending. Thanks for letting me into your life for a short time through this book. I pray that having read it, you will be blessed.

Breinigsville, PA USA
04 August 2010
242951BV00005B/13/P